RAISED *in the* KITCHEN

MAKING MEMORIES FROM SCRATCH
ONE RECIPE AT A TIME

CARRIAN CHENEY

SHADOW
MOUNTAIN

To my parents, who raised me in an
unassuming, safe kitchen.

To Cade and the kids for helping me
create a place where we can share the
love we feel for each other.

And for all of you for settling in at our
table and sharing in this journey together.
You are part of this family.

Food Photography by Carrian Cheney
Cheney Family Photography by Jessica Kettle and Aria Bethards

Visit us at shadowmountain.com

Library of Congress Cataloging-in-Publication Data
(CIP data on file)
ISBN 978-1-62972-845-2

Printed in China
RR Donnelley, Dongguan, China

10 9 8 7 6 5 4 3 2 1

CONTENTS

INTRODUCTION

You know that evening when you have just enjoyed one of the most delicious meals you've ever had, and you're perfectly, comfortably full? The sun has already set, and you've leaned back a little, the chair has become a part of you, and you're completely present. There's laughter and clinking of a few plates as someone is using the back of their fork to pick up every last crumb from dessert. The sky is dotted with stars just beginning to reveal themselves, but you don't even notice because the company is too good. The conversation has wrapped itself around your shoulders with the most enveloping pull, and you take the chance to look around at all those happy faces. The dinner could go on for hours without a scrap of food left because it's the moment that's delicious. In Spanish, there's one word that describes that moment, that feeling: *sobremesa.*

How do I even begin to tell you in this book how you'll achieve your *sobremesa*? As I'm thinking about it, I feel a burning in my heart and maybe a little in my eyes. This book will be the link. It will be that silver thread that somehow reaches its delicate fibers through time, tying your family's hearts together. It will start with the first waft of the fluffy, buttery pancakes on the griddle, sizzling and breathing as bubble after bubble bursts. Suddenly someone will be reminded of that night you stayed up late, eating pancakes at an hour when most are in bed and talking about your first breakup or how totally unfair Dad was for making you come home early. A moment woven into time.

Or it might be the feel of the soft, warm dough being pinched off and gently shaped into balls to be set aside while the griddle heats. Ahhhh, fresh tortillas are being stacked, ready for taco night, but your children's mouths will be squeezing oh so tight as they remember you getting all fancy, lifting and jerking the pan because duh, of course you can flip it one-handed. But alas, you're no Iron Chef, and the next thing you know you're chucking a tortilla Frisbee-style at the closest kid for laughing at your tortilla flopped on the ground.

Fail.

And there's that thread again, wrapping and weaving its way into their hearts. Isn't that all you've wanted all along anyway? Moments that somehow create this thing called Life.

When you're no longer there with your kids, don't you want a way to still be there? These pages, these recipes—they're your way to create a tapestry of love and unity within the walls of your own home, within the very souls you have been entrusted to care for on this earth.

One day you won't be there. But the smell of that sauce gurgling on the stove will, and there your little one will be, all grown up, stressing about the flour that exploded all over when the mixer got turned on and the eggshells that are literally crunching with each turn of the beater blade. There she is, teaching her kids the basics using these exact same recipes, just the way my mom did so many years ago for me. In fact, if I'm really quiet, if I have just a breath of being still, I'm there.

Our countertops weren't like they are now. I don't even know what it was, laminate? It was all white with the smallest amount of texture as I laid my hands on top to climb up on my oak stool. Grating cheese was my job that night, the best job of all because every five seconds I could pinch a clump of those tasty strands just begging to be eaten.

Times are a little different now. I'm not that little girl with the hair-bobble ponytail holder and perfectly rolled socks above my white Keds. Now I'm the mom. I'm the one turning up the music as I move from pot to pan, from cutting board to sink, fussing here and there to get dinner on the table—one that half of the kids won't even eat #becausegrayson. Cue the eye roll and the awkward smile as I know his picky eating was inherited from none other than me.

But there I am, moving through the kitchen as if it's a dance to the music, and if you stop and listen—really *listen*—it's the music of the kitchen that is filling my family that night. It's the sizzling of the pan, the muscle of the mixer struggling to knead a dough that has just come together. It's

the smells of the butter browning with the herbs blooming to make the best pizza sauce ever.

You see, if you learn to hear the music that plays in the joy of childhood, the love of two people, and even the sounds of the kitchen, it tells you everything to do. When it's time to hug instead of discipline. When it's time to add more to the pot so the garlic doesn't burn. When it's time to turn everything off, to step away, and to partake together because the work is done and once again the song has returned to the soft melody of the day, the family settling into chairs, tiny hands reaching for the bread before the blessing has been said.

I guess what I want to tell you is that this book isn't mine, it's yours. It's the book that will write your story with your children—your moments and memories. It's the book I never intended to write but always intended for you to have.

What was going to be a cookbook for kids written by my kids never happened. Instead, this is a book written by a mother to the mothers, the fathers, the children who are all looking to make the kitchen a place of becoming. This book is about learning to cook, about messing up and trying again. It's about creating moments, creating food, creating homes, and, in the end, it's about you.

You and I have probably never met. Your home may have been different from mine. Many of us were raised in different places all over the world, but me? I was raised in the kitchen.

I hope your children will be too.

For tips on creating pantry lists, kitchen tool recommendations, and cleaning schedules, visit me at ohsweetbasil.com

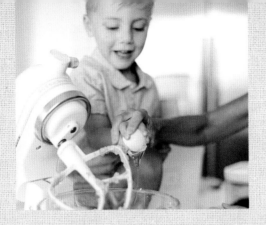

TEACHING KIDS TO COOK

Teaching your children to cook will be "the best of times and the worst of times," especially if you as the parent are learning too.

If you've ever found it funny or ironic (or both) that the word *desserts* spelled backward is *stressed*, then you also know how easy it is to go from delicious to disaster in the kitchen. There will likely be many disasters when teaching your children to cook.

I have flopped every single blueberry muffin recipe I've ever made. Oh well, someday I'll make them tall and fluffy while still soft and flavorful.

I've gotten mad at the kids and finally sent them all out of the kitchen so I could clean up their messes and finish cooking alone, only to regret my sharp tone the rest of the evening.

And on and on.

Actually, I've also made brown booger nuggets, and that wasn't good either.

I meant to write, "topped with brown sugar nuggets," but under the description on Pinterest I wrote . . . BROWN BOOGER NUGGETS.

Brown. Booger. Nuggets.

That's what I wrote. And there's no getting it back. It's out there on Pinterest forever.

I make silly mistakes, say the wrong things at the wrong time, and mess up all the time—and that goes for the kitchen too. But I think my silly mistakes actually help me teach my kids.

Please remember, it's not about perfect. It's not even about the food—it's about the souls being fed through it all. It's about time and connecting, so let the dish fail, but don't give up on your kids or yourself.

Try not to worry about cooking all the time. It's okay to start with the goal of cooking only once a week.

Set boundaries and give jobs. Do not let your kids cook everything, all the time—especially by themselves. Teach them to respect you and accept age-appropriate tasks. Start small: "You tear the lettuce while Mommy cooks the meat; I can't wait until you're bigger and using the stove will be your job."

Or just say it like my older sister did: "You can do it when you're older than me." Hah! You better believe that didn't last for very long before I caught on.

Don't stress. Just take a deep breath, stick a box of instant potatoes in the cupboard in case your mashed potatoes don't turn out, and get cooking. You get comfortable with the recipe and then let the kids help. One recipe at a time. One deep breath after another. Cooking absolutely will become easier. I promise.

Blueberry Waffles P. 13

BREAKFAST

Chocolate Smoothie Bowl

We've started this little tradition thanks to our friends Dave and Sarah. We have smoothies for dinner all the time, especially during the summer. Actually, we have smoothies and popcorn—don't judge. Hear me out on this kid-friendly smoothie bowl, then we urge you to do the same with your kids. It's healthy, smooth, and creamy, and when served with a side of popcorn, it makes the perfect treat.

Everyone should know how to make a good smoothie, not just for the nutrition, but so that we all learn to make time for every meal instead of just skipping.

Time: 5 min   *Yield:* 2 to 4 servings

1¼ cups low-fat chocolate milk

1 cup chopped frozen bananas

¼ cup vanilla Greek yogurt

½ to 1 cup fresh baby spinach

¼ cup peanut butter

1 tablespoon chia seeds

Toppings

Sliced bananas

Berries

Granola

Shredded coconut

Melted peanut butter

1. Add milk, frozen bananas, yogurt, spinach, peanut butter, and chia seeds to the jar of a blender. Process until smooth, about 1 minute.

2. Pour into bowls and top with additional fruit, granola, and coconut shreds. Drizzle melted peanut butter over top and serve.

NOTE: For extra protein, adults can add a scoop of protein powder to the smoothie as well.

Pro Tip: Try using regular milk or a different dairy alternative, as well as different types of frozen fruit, to create your own smoothie shop—like a Jamba Juice at home.

Chocolate-Dipped Waffle Cone Yogurt Cups

Let's face it, eating healthy isn't easy, especially when it comes to kids and snack time. Opting for healthy snacks that aren't junk food takes a little extra thinking and creativity. But getting your kids involved and letting them experiment in the kitchen can be a total game changer.

This is an easy recipe that you can make with kids because there's no baking or sharp utensils, and it's the perfect way for kids to get creative while learning about nutrition. Invite them to play around with flavors and textures. The more they play with food, the more they'll learn what works, what doesn't, and how to finish something all by themselves.

Prep: 10 min *Chill:* 5 min *Total:* 15 min *Yield:* 8 cones

8 (4- to 6-ounce) cups for holding the cones

8 waffle cones

1½ cups milk chocolate melting wafers (see note)

2⅔ to 4 cups vanilla yogurt (see note)

2 cups fresh berries, such as sliced strawberries, blueberries, raspberries, blackberries, or a mixture of your favorites

1. Arrange cups on a large tray or rimmed baking sheet; set aside.
2. In a microwave-safe bowl, melt chocolate on high power in 30-second increments, stirring between each increment, until smooth.
3. Dip the mouth of each waffle cone in chocolate and place cones, pointed side down, in cups. Place tray in refrigerator 5 to 10 minutes to allow chocolate to set.
4. When ready to serve, remove cones from refrigerator and fill each with ⅓ to ½ cup yogurt. Top with berries and serve immediately.

NOTE: Most supermarkets stock Ghirardelli Milk Chocolate Wafers in 10-ounce packages. But you can also use milk chocolate chips if melting chocolate is hard to come by in your area.

NOTE: You can use any flavor yogurt that pairs well with berries and chocolate. Plain yogurt mixed with a drizzle of honey is also good. To make your own yogurt, see page 32.

Peyton and Claire Tip:
We love to make these after school with friends because they're simple and quick, plus we can choose what goes in and what yogurt to use. Our favorite part—dipping in white or milk chocolate and sprinkles if it's someone's birthday.

Cinnamon Roll Oatmeal

Sometimes—most times, maybe?—oatmeal gets a bad rap for being boring or bland. But it can be turned into something fabulous in just 10 minutes. This easy recipe is one of those dishes that sets you up for success, and it means you can eat something delicious and healthy even on a busy day.

Prep: 5 min *Cook:* 5 min *Total:* 10 min *Yield:* 4 servings

2 cups old-fashioned oats

4 cups low-fat milk

½ teaspoon cinnamon

Brown Sugar Swirl

1 tablespoon unsalted butter

2 tablespoons brown sugar

⅛ teaspoon ground cinnamon

Glaze

1 tablespoon vanilla or plain Greek yogurt

2 tablespoons powdered sugar

Dash vanilla extract (optional)

1. Add oats, milk, and ½ teaspoon cinnamon to a medium saucepan. Stir briefly, then bring to a boil over medium-high heat. Reduce heat to medium-low and simmer 3 to 5 minutes, or until thickened and most of the liquid is gone. Remove pan from heat, cover with lid, and set aside.

2. Melt butter in a small, microwave-safe bowl on high power 15 to 20 seconds. Stir in brown sugar and remaining ⅛ teaspoon cinnamon and set aside.

3. In a separate small bowl, stir together Greek yogurt and powdered sugar until smooth. If desired, stir in dash of vanilla.

4. Divide oatmeal between 2 bowls. Drizzle butter-sugar mixture over top of the oatmeal, followed by a drizzle or 2 of the yogurt-sugar mixture. Serve immediately.

Blueberry Waffles

Everyone claims to have the ultimate waffle recipe, but I was bold and challenged all of those recipes to a throw down. The kids and I spent way too much time pulling up every recipe we could find for buttermilk waffles, and even more time testing all of the recipes. We even pulled out the Bobby Flay waffle recipe from his chicken and waffles throw down. It was good, but it was not the ultimate. This one is. The addition of juicy blueberries takes it right over the top.

Prep: 30 min   *Cook:* 24 min   *Total:* 54 min   *Yield:* 4 to 6 servings

1¾ cups all-purpose flour

2¼ teaspoons baking powder

¼ teaspoon baking soda

2 tablespoons cornstarch

3 tablespoons plus 1 teaspoon granulated sugar

½ teaspoon fine sea salt

3 large eggs

¾ cup buttermilk

¾ cup heavy cream

½ cup unsalted butter, melted and cooled slightly

1½ cups frozen blueberries

1. In a large bowl, whisk together flour, baking powder, baking soda, cornstarch, sugar, and salt.

2. In another bowl, whisk together the eggs, buttermilk, and heavy cream.

3. Using a wooden spoon, stir the wet ingredients into the dry ingredients until batter is almost mixed together but a few streaks of flour remain. Add melted butter and blueberries and stir until just combined. Set bowl aside to rest 15 to 30 minutes. (Do not skip the resting time.)

4. Heat waffle iron according to manufacturer's directions. Brush butter on both sides of the waffle iron. Pour ⅓ cup batter (more or less, depending on the iron) onto the iron and cook according to manufacturer's directions.

Grayson Tip:
We tried using fresh blueberries a few times, but they were a little sour and smashed up in the batter. Our secret? Use frozen blueberries, which not only are sweeter but don't get all green and mushy in the cooked waffle.

Banana Buttermilk Pancakes

We spent years and years creating the perfect pancake recipe, and not only was it so much fun to do as a family, to talk about what we liked and didn't like (I *highly* encourage you to talk about the food you're eating), but it taught our kids—and us—a lot about what works and what doesn't in cooking.

We also ate a lot of pancakes for dinner during those years—and what's better than that?

Now the kids think it's fun to take our classic recipe and mix in different ingredients or add different toppings. It's playing in the kitchen at its best, and I love it.

Prep: 10 min *Cook:* 4 min *Total:* 14 min *Yield:* 8 to 12 pancakes

2 cups sifted all-purpose flour

2 tablespoons granulated sugar

1 teaspoon salt

2 teaspoons baking powder

1 teaspoon baking soda

2 large eggs, lightly beaten

2 cups buttermilk

2 tablespoons unsalted butter, melted

1 cup sliced bananas

Claire Tip:
I think my whole family has messed up flipping things on a hot stove (my mom once flipped an entire omelet on the floor and we couldn't stop laughing; eggs were even on the walls), but my mom taught me a good tip. Use a sturdy spatula—ours is metal—and scoop quick all the way under the pancake. Flip with your wrist in one quick motion because if you slowly tilt and turn it over, it ends up a mess.

1. Preheat nonstick skillet to medium heat. (350 degrees F. on an electric griddle.)
2. In a medium bowl, whisk together flour, sugar, salt, baking powder, and baking soda; set aside.
3. In a separate bowl, whisk together eggs and buttermilk until completely combined. Drizzle in melted butter as you continue to whisk.
4. Make a well in the middle of the dry ingredients. Pour wet ingredients and bananas into the well and stir with wooden spoon until a few streaks of flour remain. (The more you stir pancake batter, the flatter and tougher the pancakes will be, so be careful not to overmix. It's okay if the batter is lumpy.)
5. Butter the griddle and use a ⅓ cup measure to portion batter onto hot griddle. Cook until bubbles begin to form and pop on top, about 2 to 3 minutes. Flip pancakes and cook until second side is golden brown, about 1 to 2 minutes. Serve immediately with Coconut Buttermilk Syrup (page 17).

Coconut Buttermilk Syrup

We've always been obsessed, as have all our readers, with the buttermilk syrup recipe on our blog. I often joke that it's like liquid gold, but really, it's the only pancake syrup I make anymore. Here's the chance to take a recipe you love and make it into something new. I took my friend Mya's advice and switched the vanilla in our syrup recipe for coconut extract, and I am beyond in love. It's so blasted good! I would bathe in it if I could (very skin clarifying, I am sure!), but then I think about cleaning the mess that would be left behind, and I guess I'll stick to just eating it. Let the drooling commence!

Prep: 5 min   *Cook:* 15 min   *Total:* 20 min   *Yield:* 2 cups

½ cup unsalted butter

1 cup granulated sugar

1 cup buttermilk

1 tablespoon light corn syrup

2 teaspoons coconut extract

1 teaspoon baking soda

1. In a large, heavy-bottomed pot or saucepan, add butter, sugar, buttermilk, and corn syrup. Bring to a boil over medium heat, stirring occasionally.

2. Remove from heat, stir in coconut extract and baking soda, then return to heat immediately, stirring constantly. At first, the syrup will bubble up and threaten to boil over, which is why a large pot is essential. If the mixture gets too high, remove pot from burner briefly and continue stirring to bring it down. Reduce heat and maintain a simmer 5 to 10 minutes, stirring occasionally, until the mixture begins to turn amber in color and thickens slightly. Serve immediately.

Grayson Tip:
Peyton is obsessed with coconut, but there are lots of extract flavors to try in the baking aisle. I want Mom to buy root beer just once!

Homemade Pancake Mix

Being prepared to make things if you can't get fresh items or can't get to the store is one of the best things you can do to feel in control of your kitchen. Freezing, prepping, or mixing ahead of time doesn't have to be some big ol' Saturday of labor. I don't have time for that. But I do have 5 minutes and a storage container.

This easy, homemade buttermilk pancake mix was born out of our most viral pancake recipe ever—our Melt in Your Mouth Buttermilk Pancakes—and the need to survive life. With just a few ingredients, you will have pancake mix on deck at all times for whenever the craving hits.

Time: 5 min (for mix) *Yield:* 5¼ cups (of mix)

4 cups sifted all-purpose flour	2 teaspoons salt
¼ cup granulated sugar	4 teaspoons baking powder
1 cup powdered buttermilk	2 teaspoons baking soda

In a large bowl, whisk together all ingredients to combine well. Store in an airtight container, such as a 4.4-quart OXO Good Grips POP container, until ready to use.

Peyton Tip:
Print the recipe for the mix and how to make the batter on sticker paper, stick it to the container, and store this in the pantry so you always have the recipe right there for you. We have a free printable on our website.

Ready to Make Pancakes?

2 eggs	3 cups pancake mix
1¼ cups water	2 tablespoons unsalted butter, melted

1. Whisk together eggs and water (see note).
2. Fold egg-water mixture into dry pancake mix until batter comes together but is not completely mixed.
3. Add melted butter and stir just to combine. Batter will be lumpy.
4. Scoop ⅓ cup of batter onto a hot, buttered griddle and cook until bubbles form on top. Flip pancakes and cook until golden on the second side. Makes about 15 small pancakes.

NOTE: You can use powdered or dehydrated eggs as well. Use 1 tablespoon egg powder to 2 tablespoons water for a single egg. Multiply accordingly.

BACON EQUALS HAPPINESS

All right, let's begin with a little math problem.

If Russell has twelve pieces of bacon and eats eight of those pieces, what does Russell have?

Happiness. Russell has happiness.

There's nothing quite like bacon: the smell, the sound of it sizzling in the pan, the popping and snapping of the grease as it explodes from the heat, the crunchy texture, the salty, savory taste. It's all pretty much amazing.

Ironically, I hated bacon as a kid. Greasy, crunchy, and fatty, often over- or undercooked, bacon was a hard pass for me.

I remember waking up one morning while camping with a number of people from our church group. I noticed that the side of our tent was just a little damp from the dew that had settled in the campground that morning. It was going to be a chilly start to the day. Fortunately, my mom had taught me the best trick: when you go to bed, put your clothes in the bottom of your sleeping bag and they will be warm all night. In the morning you can just shimmy out of your jammies and right on into your toasty warm clothes. Genius!

Carefully, I slipped into my peg-legged, acid-washed jeans and an old sweatshirt, pulled my hair through a dainty scrunchy, and managed to brush against the damp sides of the tent only half a dozen times or so. The chill of the morning rushed into the musty tent as I unzipped the door and flung open the flap.

Instantly, I could hear the distinct sounds of breakfast being made.

Who needs Christmas morning sounds when there's breakfast?

I scurried over to a huge firepit, where a little shaggy-haired boy in a puffy coat was helping his dad serve breakfast to all of the people gathered.

"You want any bacon?" he asked. He was quite polite for a nine-year-old, but I wasn't suckered in.

"Nah, I don't like bacon."

"What? Who doesn't like bacon?"

That was the moment I dug my heels in—just like the picky little eater I was.

"Me. I don't." And that was that.

It wasn't until college that I realized the glory of bacon and that people were cooking it wrong all over the world.

Let me teach you what I mean. It all starts with a cold pan. . . .

The Best Bacon

The stove-top method is the preferred one for crispy, snappy bacon. The stove top makes for a crunchier bacon because the fat slowly renders (fancy word for "melts") out of the bacon, leaving you with perfect meat, but it takes more time to do big batches. When cooking for a crowd, baking bacon in the oven is a must.

Prep: 5 min   *Cook:* 20 min   *Total:* 25 min   *Yield:* 6 servings

1 pound bacon

Stove-Top

1. Place a cast-iron skillet or nonstick pan on the stove and line it with bacon, not allowing slices to overlap.
2. Turn the burner to low (or medium if in a hurry).
3. Allow the bacon to begin cooking and use tongs to flip the bacon occasionally to ensure even cooking and browning. This can take up to 15 minutes, but most pieces are done somewhere between 8 and 12 minutes.

Oven-Baked

1. Line 2 rimmed baking sheets with aluminum foil.
2. Arrange half of the bacon on each baking sheet, making sure slices do not overlap or touch.
3. Heat oven to 400 degrees F. Bake 1 sheet at a time, 15 to 20 minutes, each. During the last 5 minutes, once the bacon is brown and sizzling, flip each piece over using tongs or a fork.
4. Transfer cooked bacon to a paper towel-lined plate.

NOTE: Check the bacon after 10 minutes as thin bacon will cook faster than thick-cut bacon.

Grayson Tip:
Sprinkle a little brown sugar on the bacon before it goes in the oven for candied bacon—my favorite kind!

Cheesy Scrambled Eggs

I will never forget being on a business trip and watching the woman at the table next to me yell at the waiter that her scrambled eggs were not runny like she'd asked for. I could see them: any runnier and they'd be literally uncooked eggs. That's reserved for cookie dough, lady. Otherwise, let's add some heat!

Everyone should learn to make eggs not only because they're a staple in American homes but also because they're a really cheap and easy way to eat when you're short on time and money (hello, college students).

Prep: 10 min   *Cook:* 5 min   *Total:* 15 min   *Yield:* 3 servings

6 large eggs

4 tablespoons milk (see note)

½ cup shredded cheddar cheese

½ teaspoon salt

Dash ground black pepper

1 to 2 tablespoons butter or oil

1. In a large bowl, whisk together the eggs, milk, cheese, salt, and pepper. Chill in refrigerator 5 to 10 minutes. This resting time allows the salt to do its work and trap some moisture in the eggs; if you don't have time to wait, proceed immediately to step 2.

2. Heat a large, nonstick skillet over medium-low heat for runnier scrambled eggs or medium-high heat for a firmer scramble. Melt butter until it foams or heat oil until it shimmers, and then quickly pour in the eggs. Allow the eggs to sit for a few seconds; then, using a rubber spatula, begin stirring the eggs until set. For a runnier scramble, stir more slowly and gently.

3. When desired texture is reached, transfer to a plate and season with a little more salt and pepper if needed.

NOTE: To serve more than 3 people, use a ratio of 2 tablespoons milk for every 3 eggs when making adjustments.

3 Secrets to Excellent Scrambled Eggs

1. Use milk, water, or even cottage cheese in the eggs. Adding liquid acts as a barrier and will keep the eggs from grabbing each other in cooking and getting dried out and rubbery.

2. Salt the eggs (¼ teaspoon per 3 eggs) and let them sit up to 15 minutes before cooking. This allows the salt to dissolve some proteins in the eggs so not as much moisture will be lost, and you'll be left with softer, melt-in-your-mouth eggs.

3. Use high heat unless you're looking for runny eggs (which I know some like, so that's okay). A quick blast of high heat will cook those eggs up without leaving them time to get chewy.

The Best French Toast

I've loved French toast my whole life. Especially when we get to have breakfast for dinner. I seriously think there's nothing better than a thick slice of French toast piled with juicy strawberries, drizzled with thick syrup, and maybe even dusted with powdered sugar.

Just for you, I tested so many recipes for French toast that our kids finally asked for chicken for dinner just to change things up. The secret to the best French toast? Well, take a peek at Peyton's tip, as she was my partner in crime for discovering the best recipe.

Prep: 5 min   *Cook:* 5 min   *Total:* 10 min   *Yield:* 6 slices

Peyton Tip:

The best bread to use is a thick, dense bread like brioche or challah. Our local grocery store makes both, but if you can't find it, you can use Texas toast or even French bread.

Next up is the egg mixture. My mom says she grew up with just egg and milk, but I hate it when there's thick egg whites stuck all over the bread. Instead, making a batter with egg, milk, flour, and sugar gives you the best French toast. And a dash of cinnamon? Well, now you're just showing off, and my mom always approves of showing off in the kitchen, unless she's the cook—then you better let her have the limelight.

1 large egg

2 tablespoons butter, melted, plus more for greasing griddle

¾ cup whole milk

2 teaspoons vanilla extract

2 tablespoons granulated sugar

⅓ cup all-purpose flour

Dash ground cinnamon (optional)

Dash ground nutmeg (optional)

¼ teaspoon salt

1 loaf brioche or challah bread, sliced 1-inch thick

1. Beat egg in a shallow baking dish or pie plate. Briskly whisk in melted butter, followed by milk and vanilla. Add sugar, flour, cinnamon, nutmeg, and salt, whisking until smooth. Set aside.

2. Heat a large nonstick griddle to 350 degrees F. and spread butter all over the bottom.

3. Working with 1 slice of bread at a time, soak bread in batter 15 to 20 seconds per side. Transfer to hot griddle and cook 1 minute. Flip the bread, cooking on the other side until golden, about 1 more minute. Serve with Coconut Buttermilk Syrup (page 17).

Croissant Breakfast Sandwich

Are you a sweet or savory breakfast person? I'm totally into both, depending on the day.

Our friends once mentioned to us that we should try our favorite breakfast sandwiches—which are typically savory—on croissants, with a mustard and maple sauce. I was up for the challenge to mix a little something sweet with the savory and enlisted the kids to help. Thus Croissant Breakfast Sandwiches were born!

Prep: 10 min   *Cook:* 20 min   *Total:* 30 min   *Yield:* 6 sandwiches

1 pound ground maple breakfast
  sausage

2 tablespoons mayonnaise

2 tablespoons yellow or Dijon mustard

2 tablespoons pure maple syrup

8 large eggs

¼ cup milk

1 cup shredded Colby Jack cheese

Salt and ground black pepper, to taste

6 croissants, split horizontally

6 strips bacon, cooked (page 21)

Minced chives, for garnishing

1. Form breakfast sausage into 6 rectangular patties to better fit onto the croissants. Cook sausage patties in a large skillet over medium heat until cooked through, about 7 to 8 minutes per side. When cooked through, remove from heat and cover with lid to keep warm until sandwiches are ready to assemble.

2. While sausage cooks, prepare sauce and mix together the ingredients for scrambled eggs. For sauce: whisk together mayonnaise, mustard, and maple syrup in a small bowl; set aside until ready to assemble sandwiches. For eggs: in a large bowl, whisk together eggs, milk, cheese, salt, and pepper. Set aside in refrigerator while sausage finishes cooking.

3. Heat oven to broil. Place croissant halves, open sides up, on baking sheet and toast under broiler until golden brown, about 1 to 2 minutes; set aside until ready to assemble sandwiches.

4. Heat a small amount of butter or oil in a nonstick skillet over medium heat. (Alternatively, use nonstick cooking spray.) When pan is hot, pour egg mixture into skillet, let mixture sit a minute or so, then use a rubber spatula to stir and fold until eggs are cooked and scrambled, about 3 to 5 minutes. Remove from heat.

5. Assemble sandwiches: Use 1 tablespoon sauce, a spoonful or 2 of the scrambled eggs, 1 sausage patty, 1 strip bacon, and a sprinkle of chopped chives for each sandwich.

Sausage-Hash Brown Casserole

One night, just after I turned twelve, I was sleeping soundly in my bed (picture a scrawny little thing, with mousy brown hair, the snaggliest teeth in all the world, and a jaw widener shoved in her mouth), when I was jolted awake by the creak of a door. I groggily opened my eyes, ready to eat my little sister alive if she was waking me up early, and was shocked to see a gaggle of friends instead. They'd arrived in the wee hours of the morning with a casserole for a surprise birthday breakfast celebration.

This cheesy breakfast casserole is full of flavor, but it also combines your skills with eggs and sausage, multitasking, preparing a recipe, and finally baking it off.

Prep: 20 min   *Cook:* 40 min   *Total:* 1 hour   *Yield:* 12 servings

4 large eggs

1 cup milk

½ teaspoon salt

Pinch ground black pepper

1 pound ground maple-sage breakfast sausage

¼ cup minced onion

1 (15-ounce) bag frozen shredded hash browns

1 cup shredded sharp cheddar cheese

1 cup shredded mozzarella cheese

Fresh coarsely ground black pepper

1. Preheat oven to 350 degrees F. Spray an 8x8-inch baking dish with nonstick cooking spray.

2. In a medium bowl, whisk together eggs, milk, salt, and pepper until thoroughly combined; set aside. (Allowing the egg mixture to rest gives the salt in the mixture time to break down the eggs and thus create a fluffier baked egg dish.)

3. In a large skillet over medium heat, cook and break up sausage with a wooden spoon until almost all of the pink is gone. Add onions and cook, stirring occasionally, until soft and translucent, 3 to 4 minutes. Using a slotted spoon, remove the meat

Multitasking in the Kitchen

Always scan a recipe for what can be done in advance and set aside, like shredding the cheese and storing it in the fridge until you need to use it.

Croissants can be sliced open and stored in zip-top bags the night before; most sauces can be whisked up and stored in the fridge up to a week in advance.

Learn to rely on your nose and ears. When first trying a dish, definitely set a timer according to the recipe's directions. But then really pay attention to your nose and ears to learn the music of the kitchen. Is something sizzling? It's probably time to check on it. Does that butter you're browning suddenly smell nutty and rich? It's probably time to take it off the heat. Soon, timers will become secondary, and you'll be able to cook several things at once, distinguishing when it's time for the next step by simply listening and sniffing.

and onions to a plate. Leave behind the cooking grease from the sausage, as it will be used to brown the hash browns.

4. If needed, add enough cooking oil to the hot sausage grease in the skillet to cover the bottom of the pan. Add hash browns to hot skillet and cook until lightly browned, 4 to 6 minutes. Flip and cook on the other side an additional 4 minutes.

5. Transfer hash browns to prepared baking dish. Top with sausage and half of each cheese. Pour egg mixture over the top and sprinkle with remaining cheese. Sprinkle some fresh coarsely ground black pepper over the top and bake 35 to 40 minutes, or until set and golden.

NOTE: This dish can be prepped in advance. Once assembled, cover pan tightly with aluminum foil and refrigerate up to 12 hours. Remove from refrigerator and let dish rest 15 minutes before baking.

THE PLANT EXPERIMENT

It's pretty easy for me to want to be the teacher in the kitchen; I'm the all-knowing adult. But as my kids have grown, they've had ideas of their own, like my daughter who randomly soaked garlic in water to peel it and BLEW MY MIND with how easy it was. I look back at my own mom, who has always been willing to learn something from me, and I think maybe there's a secret in that.

I remember a lesson Claire taught our family about service. She asked everyone to share one thing that they thought they could do to serve a family member. Each person gave great answers, and then she said, "Can I share mine? No one has said it."

She proceeded to tell us that in school she had learned about two plants. Every day one plant was told how beautiful and good it was, that its leaves were the perfect shade of green, and it would one day be so big and tall.

The second plant was told that it was ugly, small, and worthless, that its leaves were uneven and broken, and on and on.

By the end of the experiment, the first plant was alive, healthy, strong, and beautiful. The second plant was brown, withered, and dying.

And Claire said this: "I think the best service we can give in our home is to think and say kind things to and about each other."

What a wise, sweet little girl. How often it's the ones we love the most whom we are quickest to become angry with, the slowest to express love to, and the likeliest to think ungrateful or mean thoughts about. Even with our children, how often in our minds do we think, "Ugh, you're driving me crazy!" And although that may be true in the moment, what if we thought and said only the very best about each other?

Every day, each person starts out as an empty jar. Every word fills up that jar with good things or destructive things.

If nothing else, I hope that when my life is over, the people I knew can stand before me and say, "I knew she loved me, and some days that was enough."

Instant Pot Yogurt

In college, I had a ridiculously tiny food budget. When yogurt would go on sale, I'd buy a few cartons and consider it my splurge on groceries. (It's the little things, guys.)

Despite my limited food budget, I loved being on my own. But one thing I hated was trying to figure out how to cook for just one person. I so wish I'd had an Instant Pot back then to make quick, small meals. It's my number-one suggestion for college students to bring with them if they live in an apartment-style setting.

This homemade Instant Pot yogurt recipe requires less than 5 minutes of hands-on prep work and uses just 3 ingredients. The yogurt stores well in the refrigerator for weeks.

Prep: 5 min *Inactive:* 1 to 4 hours *Cook:* 9+ hours *Total:* 10+ hours *Yield:* 12 cups

1 gallon whole or 2 percent milk

3 tablespoons plain Greek yogurt with active cultures

1 teaspoon vanilla extract

Honey, for serving

1. Pour the entire gallon of milk into the insert of an Instant Pot.

2. Secure lid, press the Yogurt button, and adjust settings until digital readout displays "Boil." (The vent does not need to be closed.) Depending on the make and model of your Instant Pot, press the Start button or simply allow the cycle to begin automatically. It will take about an hour for the milk to heat to correct temperature.

3. When Instant Pot signals the end of this stage, carefully remove the lid and check the temperature of the milk on an instant read thermometer. It must be between 180 degrees F. and 200 degrees F. If it is lower than 180 degrees F., whisk milk briefly, then press the Sauté button and heat, stirring frequently, until milk reaches 180 degrees F.

4. Remove the inner pot and place it on a trivet or hot pad on the counter to cool until milk reaches 110 degrees F., about 1 hour. Carefully remove any skin that forms on the top and discard. Whisk in the 3 tablespoons yogurt.

5. Return insert to Instant Pot, secure lid, and press the Yogurt button. (Again, the vent does not need to be closed.) Adjust incubation time to 8 hours. For a tangier yogurt, increase time to 10 hours or more.

6. When the Instant Pot signals the end of incubation, remove lid and stir in vanilla. Remove insert and let yogurt cool to room temperature before transferring to an airtight container and refrigerating. To make Greek yogurt, strain yogurt by lining a fine sieve with cheesecloth or a coffee filter and setting the sieve over a bowl. Spoon yogurt into sieve and refrigerate the bowl and sieve together 2 hours to allow the liquid to drain off. Transfer to an airtight container and refrigerate to store.

7. Serve yogurt drizzled with honey.

Garlic Parmesan Focaccia Bread P. 42

BREAD

BAKING BREAD 101

My mom has always made the best bread in the whole world, and she's the one who taught me there's nothing better than slicing off a warm piece. Can't you just smell it?

Making homemade bread—whether it's a quick bread or a yeast bread—might feel like a challenge, but once you learn a few fundamental terms and tricks, it will start to feel as easy as, well, as easy as sliced bread.

QUICK BREADS

Folding, which is frequently called for in quick breads, means to carefully combine two different mixtures, usually a thicker one (such as pancake batter) with one that's lighter or airier (such as beaten egg whites) into a smooth mixture. Try folding by scraping down the sides of the bowl using a rubber spatula, pulling the spatula under the mixture, and then lifting the two mixtures together, turning them over the top like you're folding a sandwich in half. Continue until the two mixtures are combined and the consistency is still airy.

Quick breads are super easy to make because they don't rely on yeast like other bread recipes do. They are also the perfect way to test how doneness feels in a bread recipe. Here's a primer:

Don't open and shut the oven door while your bread is baking. Hot air leaving the oven and cool air entering it can make the bread fall.

After 50 minutes of baking in a regular-sized loaf pan, our banana bread will be set up enough that you can open the oven and cover the top with foil to keep it from overbrowning as it continues to bake. But first, use three fingers to gently tap the bread, pressing down to see if the top sinks at all. If it springs back up, the bread is cooked through. If it sinks, it's still doughy inside and needs another 10 minutes in the oven. It will likely take 60 minutes to be ready, but if you feel it at 50 minutes and again at 60 minutes, you'll learn the difference between uncooked and cooked bread.

Try out your new skills on Banana Bread (page 39) or Chocolate Banana Bread (page 40)!

YEAST BREADS

Yeast is a living thing. Before you use it for the first time, try seeing it in action: Fill two small bowls or glass measuring cups with 1 cup warm water each. Add 2 teaspoons instant yeast to the first bowl, give it a quick stir, and then set it aside. In the second bowl, add 1 teaspoon sugar and 2 teaspoons instant yeast, and give it a quick stir. Does one grow bigger or faster than the other? How cool is it that you just made something grow that looked like sand? What you've just done is called "proofing" the yeast.

The two types of yeast you can buy are instant yeast and active dry yeast.

Instant yeast, also called rapid rise or bread machine yeast, can be added directly to other recipe ingredients, providing they aren't too hot. Instant yeast tends to be a bit stronger than active dry yeast, so dough usually rises a little more quickly when you use it.

Although instant yeast doesn't need to proof, I always proof it anyway, because it reassures me the yeast is still alive. *Yeast is dead if it doesn't start to foam and bubble in warm water when proofed.* If it doesn't proof, I can simply throw it out and get some fresh yeast; no wasting the other ingredients. Plus, isn't it so fun to watch the yeast grow? It's like a tiny science experiment every time.

Active dry yeast should always be proofed (to activate it) in warm water before using it. Adding a little sugar for the yeast to eat makes it grow bigger and faster. Remember, if it doesn't foam and grow, it's not fresh and shouldn't be used.

Instant and active dry yeasts can be used interchangeably. I choose to work with instant yeast because I don't like taking the chance that the yeast will be finicky, which can happen with active dry yeast.

Note: Always use warm water in yeast recipes, as too-cold or too-hot water will kill the yeast.

KNEADING BREAD

When you mix flour and water together, the proteins—think of them as threads in the flour—loop through each other to form a gluten network, kind of like a spider making a web to support itself. Every time you push and fold the dough, it creates a new line in the web, making it stronger. This weblike structure is what gives bread dough the strength and elasticity it needs to grow fluffy, soft, and chewy when baked. If you don't knead, Charlotte's web will have holes in it, and when you pick up a slice, it will crumble to pieces.

However, every dough is different. Some doughs need to have the gluten worked more than others. For example, the pizza dough recipe you'll learn needs to rest a little and then be kneaded a little, while other doughs will be kneaded Swedish-massage style, over and over until the dough becomes soft, silky, and perfect for a squishy loaf of bread.

Here are the basics of kneading: On a floured surface, and with floured hands, grab one side of a ball of dough, fold it in half toward you (try pretending it's a PB&J sandwich and you're folding the bread over to eat it). With the heel of your hand, push the dough down and away from you in a smooth, rolling motion. Continue kneading until the dough is smooth and no longer sticky.

RISING

Remember how you watched the yeast get all fluffy and bubbly in the water? (You did that after reading the section on yeast, right?) Well, that's what is happening when you let the dough rise—the yeast is busy eating the sugars in the dough and creating air bubbles, making the dough rise and rise, becoming puffier and puffier. If it doesn't rise, it's a flatbread.

The White Bread recipe on page 56 is the perfect way to practice kneading as well as watching how bread rises.

Banana Bread

I seriously became obsessed with finding a perfectly moist, tender loaf of banana bread that had all the flavor without the random mix-ins. I've made more than one hundred banana bread recipes over the course of three years in search of the very best, and I've finally found it and am ready to share it with you! It smells and tastes like banana bread from heaven!

Prep: 10 min   *Cook:* 1 hour   *Total:* 1 hour 10 min   *Yield:* 1 loaf

2 cups all-purpose flour

1 teaspoon baking soda

½ teaspoon salt

⅓ cup canola oil

1 cup granulated sugar

2 large eggs

1⅓ cups mashed banana (about 2 very large or 3 small bananas)

⅔ cup mini chocolate chips

1. Preheat oven to 350 degrees F. Spray a 9x5-inch loaf pan with nonstick cooking spray.

2. In a medium bowl, whisk together flour, baking soda, and salt. Set aside.

3. In a large bowl, whisk together oil and sugar. Add eggs and whisk briefly, just to combine. Do not overmix.

4. Add dry ingredients, mashed banana, and chocolate chips to wet ingredients and gently fold together with rubber spatula or wooden spoon until just a few streaks of flour remain.

5. Pour batter into prepared pan and bake 1 hour, tenting with foil for the last 10 minutes. Touch the top, and if it doesn't leave an indentation or sink in, it's done.

6. When finished, open oven door, turn off oven, and let banana bread rest 2 to 3 minutes (no longer than that) before carefully transferring to a wire rack.

7. Cool 3 minutes, then slide a knife around the edges of pan and carefully turn the bread out into your other hand or onto the cooling rack.

8. Cool on wire rack or slice and serve warm. To store, wrap cooled loaf tightly in plastic wrap. It will keep 2 to 3 days.

Pro Tip: After spraying the pan with cooking spray, take a paper towel and wipe off ½ to 1 inch around the upper edge of the pan. As the banana bread rises, it will come in contact with the dry edge of the pan and grip it. And instead of the sides rising, just the very middle will rise into a perfect dome. This is why you don't fill muffin tins to the very top either.

Chocolate Banana Bread

It didn't take us long after discovering the very best banana bread recipe to decide to make the very best double *chocolate* banana bread recipe. You're welcome. After learning a base recipe, I always try experimenting in small ways. This is how I learned that cocoa powder on its own will dry out a recipe. Making chocolate a key ingredient means you have to play with the moisture a bit. In this recipe, we added sour cream to keep it moist.

Prep: 10 min   *Cook:* 1 hour   *Total:* 1 hour 10 min   *Yield:* 1 loaf

2 cups all-purpose flour

½ cup cocoa powder

1¼ teaspoons baking soda

½ teaspoon salt

⅓ cup canola oil

1 cup granulated sugar

5 tablespoons sour cream, at room temperature (see note)

2 large eggs, at room temperature (see note)

1¼ cups mashed banana (about 2 very large or 3 small bananas)

1 cup mini chocolate chips, divided

Claire Tip:

I love making banana bread, but I especially like trying new ways to make it. Try my chocolate version and then try other things, like adding peanut butter chips—or even cinnamon sugar on top like a snickerdoodle.

1. Preheat oven to 350 degrees F. Spray a 9x5-inch bread pan with nonstick cooking spray.

2. In a large bowl, sift together flour, cocoa powder, baking soda, and salt. Set aside.

3. In a medium bowl, whisk together oil and sugar. Add sour cream and eggs and whisk again.

4. Add wet ingredients, mashed bananas, and all but 1 to 2 tablespoons chocolate chips to the dry ingredients and gently fold together with a rubber spatula. Do not overmix.

5. Pour batter into prepared pan and sprinkle top with remaining chocolate chips. Bake 1 hour, tenting with foil for the last 10 minutes. Touch the top, and if it doesn't leave an indentation or sink in, it's done.

6. Remove from oven. Cool 2 minutes and then turn out onto a cooling rack to finish cooling.

7. Serve warm with a swipe of butter. To store, wrap cooled loaf tightly in plastic wrap. It will keep 2 to 3 days.

NOTE: This recipe turns out best when all ingredients are the same temperature. Ideally, set them out on the counter 30 to 40 minutes before prepping the recipe. If you forget, 10 minutes should be sufficient.

Garlic Parmesan Focaccia Bread

Cooking is one of the few things that takes every single sense you've got. I love that about it! The aromas and sounds, the feels and tastes of the kitchen are bouncing through the air, and the more you hear their music, the better you become at cooking. I like to teach my kids about that as we prance our fingers over the oily dough and inhale it all in.

Focaccia bread is a flat, oven-baked yeast bread that originated in Italy and is pronounced "fuh-KA-cha." It is traditionally topped with fresh herbs, such as rosemary, and coarse salt, but it is a very versatile bread that can be altered to your liking.

Prep: 10 min *Rest:* 10 hours *Cook:* 22 min *Total:* 10 hours 32 min *Yield:* 10 servings

2 cups flour (bread flour or all-purpose is fine)

1 teaspoon kosher salt

1 cup warm water

1⅛ teaspoons instant yeast

½ teaspoon granulated sugar

Olive oil

3 cloves garlic, minced

⅔ cup freshly grated Parmesan cheese

1½ teaspoons Italian seasoning

Flaked sea salt

1. In a glass bowl, combine flour and salt.
2. In a glass measuring cup, mix the warm water, yeast, and sugar. Allow to sit for a minute and then stir into the flour with a wooden spoon until the dough just comes together.
3. Cover the bowl tightly with plastic wrap and place in the fridge for 8 hours or overnight.
4. Remove the bowl from the fridge.
5. In an 8-inch round cake pan, drizzle oil and place the dough in the center, tucking ends under.
6. Cover with plastic wrap and allow to rise 2 hours.
7. Heat the oven to 450 degrees F.
8. Once risen, the dough should fill the pan. Drizzle with additional oil and use your fingers to press holes down to the bottom of the pan but not through the dough.
9. Mix garlic, cheese, and Italian seasoning in a bowl.
10. Sprinkle the dough with the garlic mixture and sea salt.
11. Place in the oven and turn down to 425 degrees F. Bake 22 to 24 minutes or until golden.

Tortillas

My friend Shelly grew up in Mexico and has always made tortillas for her family. Coming in after a date, the kids can pull up a chair in the kitchen to talk to Mom while nibbling on a warm tortilla. After-school snack after a superlong day? Shelly gets an overwhelmed kid talking by rolling out those bubbly circles of deliciousness. She has created a safe, comforting tradition that lets her family know she's there, wants to listen, and loves them.

It's her glue: tortillas, mom, kids.

The best part about cooking is finding your recipe: the one that you can whip up without thinking about it, that's quick and easy and warm and inviting. What's going to be your thing?

Prep: **10 min**   *Rest:* **15 min**   *Cook:* **2 min**   *Total:* **27 min**   *Yield:* **12 tortillas**

---

6 cups bread flour (see note)

3 teaspoons salt

4 teaspoons baking powder

⅔ cup plus 2 tablespoons canola or vegetable oil

2¼ cups boiling water

1. In the bowl of a stand mixer fitted with a dough hook, combine flour, salt, baking powder, and oil. Mix on low speed until a dough forms and resembles barely wet sand. You'll know it's ready when you can squeeze it in your hand and have the dough hold together.

2. With mixer on low, add boiling water, ½ cup at a time. Once dough is combined, mix on low another 2 to 4 minutes until dough is satiny.

3. Lightly flour or grease your hands. Remove dough to counter, then pinch off a piece of dough just smaller than the palm of your hand. In your hands, knead the dough a few times to form a rounded disc. Place disc in a greased bowl. Repeat until all dough is used. Cover bowl with a warm, damp paper towel and rest at least 10 to 15 minutes, or up to an hour.

4. When ready to cook, heat a cast-iron pan or griddle to medium heat. On a lightly floured work surface, roll out the dough balls into circles one at a time with a rolling pin until very thin.

5. Cook tortillas on hot griddle until bubbles form and

Tortilla Tips

• A tortilla warmer is absolutely worth it. You can cook your tortillas in the afternoon and they will still be warm at dinner.

• To store homemade tortillas, place a paper towel in a gallon-sized zip-top bag, add the tortillas, and place another paper towel on top before sealing shut. You can then keep them in the fridge or freezer.

• Recommended Recipes: Smothered Chicken Burritos (page 149) and Teriyaki Chicken Quesadilla (page 141).

grow large, about a minute or so, depending on your pan. Flip over and cook again until light browning shows.

6. Remove from heat and keep in a tortilla warmer lined with paper towels until ready to serve.

NOTE: Bread flour has a different amount of gluten than all-purpose flour, so it makes the tortilla hold together extra tight. You can use all-purpose flour, but the results will be different.

Grayson Tip:
I love tortillas! I like to eat the very first one we cook, hot with cheese.

Claire Tip:
I like to eat them with butter and cinnamon-sugar mix. It's one of my favorite treats.

Cornbread

I know, cornbread differs depending on the region you're from, but I have to stick with my northern roots and go sweet all the way!

This homemade, moist, sweet cornbread goes perfectly with Slow Cooker Broccoli Cheese Soup (page 126) or Chicken Tortilla Soup (page 134). It's northern sweet cornbread at its finest.

Prep: 10 min *Cook:* 45 min *Total:* 55 min *Yield:* 12 to 15 servings

1 cup Bisquick baking mix

3½ tablespoons cornmeal

½ cup granulated sugar

3 teaspoons all-purpose flour

1½ teaspoons baking powder

¼ teaspoon salt

3 large eggs, lightly beaten

¾ cup unsalted butter, melted

½ cup honey

1 cup milk

½ teaspoon vanilla extract

1 recipe To Die For Honey Butter (page 49)

1. Preheat oven to 400 degrees F. Spray a 9x9-inch baking pan with nonstick cooking spray. Alternatively, use a 9x13-inch pan (the cornbread will be less thick), but do not use an 8x8-inch pan.

2. In a large bowl, whisk together Bisquick mix, cornmeal, sugar, flour, baking powder, and salt.

3. In a separate bowl, combine eggs, butter, honey, milk, and vanilla, stirring until smooth.

4. Add the wet ingredients to the dry ingredients and stir gently with a rubber spatula until combined. Do not overmix.

5. Pour batter into prepared baking pan and bake 15 minutes. At this point, barely open the oven door, slide a piece of aluminum foil over the bread, close the door, and bake another 20 to 25 minutes, or until the sides are set and there's barely any wiggle in the middle. It will set up more as it cools. Use the same baking time for a 9x13-inch pan.

6. When finished, open oven door, turn off oven, and let the cornbread rest 5 minutes in the oven before removing.

7. Let cornbread cool 15 minutes before cutting and serving with To Die For Honey Butter.

Pro Tip: Cornbread can be a tricky bread to tackle only because it browns quickly and sets up a little more as it's cooling, which can make it confusing to know when it's done. Fifteen minutes into baking, place a piece of aluminum foil over the top to solve the issue of overbrowning as the cornbread continues to bake.

To Die For Honey Butter

Time: 5 min   *Yield:* 1½ cups; serving size, 1 tablespoon

½ cup honey

½ cup heavy cream

½ cup granulated sugar

¾ cup unsalted butter, softened

1. In a medium saucepan over medium heat, bring the honey, heavy cream, and sugar to a boil, stirring often. Remove from heat.
2. Put butter in the jar of a blender, pour the hot cream and sugar mixture over the butter, and process until smooth.
3. Store in an airtight container in the refrigerator to cool the butter before using (at least 30 minutes). Butter can also be made up to 1 week in advance.

Cheese Bread Doodles

Whenever we order pizza, the first thing our kids want to know is, are we getting cheese bread? I'm always a big yes. HECK. YES! I know you're not going to believe this, but I actually love cheese bread even more than pizza. You can use this dough for pizza, too.

Prep: 30 min   *Rest:* 30 min   *Cook:* 10 min   *Total:* 1 hour 10 min   *Yield:* 12 rolls

4½ cups all-purpose flour

1½ teaspoons instant yeast

½ teaspoon salt

¼ cup granulated sugar

1½ nickel-sized drops liquid soy lecithin (see note)

2 cups warm (100 degrees F.) water

4 cups shredded mozzarella cheese

1. In the bowl of a stand mixer fitted with a dough hook, mix flour, yeast, salt, and sugar to combine. Add soy lecithin and mix again.
2. With the mixer on low, slowly add warm water and mix 2 minutes, until dough is smooth and pulls entirely away from sides of mixing bowl. Cover bowl with a towel and let dough rest 30 minutes.
3. Line a baking sheet with parchment paper.
4. On a lightly floured work surface, roll dough into a large rectangle. Sprinkle heavily with mozzarella cheese and roll up like you would cinnamon rolls. Cut into 1½- to 2-inch slices with unflavored dental floss or a serrated bread knife and place on prepared baking sheet.
5. Bake until golden brown, about 10 minutes.
6. Remove from oven and, while hot, brush with Garlic Butter.

Garlic Butter

4 tablespoons unsalted butter, melted

1½ to 2 teaspoons garlic seasoning with parsley, such as Johnny's Garlic Spread and Seasoning

Pizza Sauce, for dipping (page 110)

1. Combine melted butter and garlic seasoning in small bowl and brush over tops of hot cheese doodles. Serve with pizza sauce for dipping.

NOTE: Soy lecithin helps two ingredients stick together—like interlocking Lego® bricks—making a better dough that holds up and doesn't break. But if you can't find it in the baking aisle of your grocery store, it's okay to skip it.

Claire Tip:
These are so fun to make with friends because everyone can make their own version with different cheeses, or you can even try a dessert version with Nutella. But my secret is using unflavored floss to cut perfect pieces without smashing the dough. My grandma taught me that.

Dinner Rolls

Sunday dinner was always a really big deal at my house when I was a little girl. I have perfect memories of my mom in her apron and Sunday dress bustling around the kitchen to get the pot roast in the oven before church, with me on Jell-O duty. As I got older, I took on different jobs, like peeling potatoes or browning the roast. Dinner rolls, though—that was intimidating.

Not anymore! It was super important to me that we tackle yeast bread in this cookbook, but there's a reason we are making rolls before bread even though it's the same recipe. It's easier to shape and test for doneness on a roll than a big loaf of bread.

Prep: 1 hour 15 min *Rest:* 2 hours 30 min *Cook:* 20 min
Total: 4 hours 5 min *Yield:* 42 rolls

---

2 cups milk

¼ cup unsalted butter, plus more for brushing tops

2 cups water

½ cup granulated sugar

½ cup honey

3 tablespoons instant yeast

¼ cup vegetable oil

2 tablespoons fine sea salt

¾ cup evaporated milk

1 large egg, beaten

9 to 11 cups all-purpose flour

1. Heat milk in a large saucepan over medium heat just until it starts to foam around the edges. Do not boil. Add butter, water, sugar, and honey and stir until the butter has melted. Remove from heat and cool to lukewarm (105 to 115 degrees F.).

2. Sprinkle yeast over lukewarm milk mixture and then stir to combine. Pour into the bowl of a stand mixer fitted with a dough hook and let rest until foamy, 3 to 5 minutes.

3. Add oil, salt, evaporated milk, and egg and mix to combine. Add 8 cups of the flour and mix on low until dough begins coming together. Add remaining flour, ¼ cup at a time, and mix until dough pulls away from the sides of the bowl and comes together in a ball around the hook, about 5 minutes. (You may need as little as 1 cup more of flour; don't worry if not all 11 cups are used.) Remove bowl from mixer,

How to Scald Milk

Scalded milk changes how a dough turns out. It makes for a softer, squishier bread. I'll save you from the science lesson, but here's what you do:

Heat milk in a saucepan over medium heat. Be watching for foamy bubbles around the sides and a thin layer of skin on top of the milk. You can touch the top with a wooden spoon very gently and it will lift off.

Now, set it all aside to let it cool. Stick your clean finger in it occasionally to see if it feels like a warm bath. Once it does, you're ready to cruise!

The Raspberry Sweet Rolls on page 213 also use scalded milk.

Dinner Rolls *(continued)*

Peyton Tip:

This is one of the first recipes my mom let me make for Sunday dinner. She taught me that the dough can be made a day ahead, shaped, and stored in the fridge, and then you just pull it out onto the counter to rest before baking.

cover with a clean cloth, and let rise 1 to 2 hours, or until doubled in size.

4. Turn out dough onto a well-floured work surface and flip it over once or twice so it isn't sticky. Pinch off dough pieces to form golf ball–sized balls. Place shaped rolls on Silpat, parchment, or greased baking sheets. Cover and allow to rise 1 to 2 hours, or until doubled.

5. Bake at 350 degrees F. 18 to 20 minutes, until tops are golden brown and no longer doughy. Brush rolls with melted butter while they are still hot. Rolls can be stored in plastic wrap or bread bags up to 1 week.

YOU'RE GOING TO FAIL

How's that for a heading in a book meant to encourage you to cook?

But it's true: you're going to mess up sometimes. And that's okay. There never were mistakes in my mom's kitchen. She encouraged and encouraged, and we were clueless we were ruining the whole dish. I watch her doing the same thing with my children now, and I can't help but think of all my mistakes and where I'd be if I had stopped cooking.

Once I put a whole pork butt in the oven at 3:20 a.m. so it could cook all night, only to discover in the morning that I'd preheated the top oven but placed the roast in the lower oven.

Whomp. Whomp. Whomp.

Do you really ever learn if you don't have some mistakes? How did someone know to cook a pork butt for longer if the first person hadn't accidentally left it in too long and discovered it was even better?! Or what about the guy who cooked eggs for too long and discovered what leather is? Hello—someone had to mess up in order to find the better way!

It doesn't matter how bad you are in the kitchen. I do not care that you Googled how to boil water! (I might be smiling about it, but I don't think less of you.) I've Googled lots over the years: What's the difference between a clove and a bulb of garlic? How do I knead bread? Is gray meat okay to eat still? (Lol. Don't. It's not.)

You don't have to believe in yourself yet—that will come. For now, just know that I believe in you, and let that be enough.

White Bread

My mom has always made the best bread in the whole world, but this recipe is one I created. Whenever I make bread in my own kitchen, I'm somehow transported back to my childhood kitchen. I remember watching my mom kneading the dough, her long, thin fingers working the dough on the countertop, the dough smoothly spreading across the palm of her hand. With one swoosh and a fold of her wrist, she's suddenly pressing it out in a new direction. Over and over, small particles of flour dust rise and fall as if they are the very breath of the bread. It's alive, she's creating it, and I'm mesmerized.

Prep: 1 hour 15 min *Rest:* 2 hours 30 min
Cook: 30 min *Total:* 4 hours 15 min *Yield:* 3 loaves

2 cups milk

¼ cup butter, plus more for brushing tops

2 cups water

½ cup granulated sugar

½ cup honey

3 tablespoons instant yeast

¼ cup vegetable oil

2 tablespoons fine sea salt

¾ cup evaporated milk

1 large egg, beaten

9 to 11 cups all-purpose flour

1. Heat milk in a large saucepan over medium heat just until it starts to foam around the edges. Do not boil. Add butter, water, sugar, and honey and stir until the butter has melted. Remove from heat and cool to lukewarm (105 to 115 degrees F.).

2. Sprinkle yeast over lukewarm milk mixture and then stir to combine. Pour into the bowl of a stand mixer fitted with a dough hook and let rest until foamy, 3 to 5 minutes.

3. Add oil, salt, evaporated milk, and egg and mix to combine. Add 8 cups of the flour and mix on low until dough begins coming together. Add remaining flour, ¼ cup at a time, and mix until dough pulls away from the sides of the bowl and comes together in a ball around the hook, about 5 minutes. (You may need as little as 1 cup more of the flour; don't worry if not all 11 cups are used.) Remove bowl from mixer, cover with a clean cloth, and let rise 1 to 2 hours, or until doubled in size.

4. Turn out dough onto a well-floured work surface and flip it over once or twice so it isn't sticky. Divide and shape into 3 loaves. (Shape the loaves by pressing each into a rectangle and then, starting at the short end, rolling the dough into a log.) Place in greased loaf pans, cover with a towel, and let rise until doubled, about 1 hour.

5. Bake at 350 degrees F. 28 to 32 minutes, until tops are golden brown. Brush loaves with melted butter while they are still hot. Cooled loaves can be stored in plastic wrap or bread bags up to 1 week.

Italian Pasta Salad P. 79

SIDES

Baked Potatoes

Shhhhhh, do not tell anyone my weird secret. I ate my baked potatoes with ketchup growing up. Okay, I lied—I still do it. You guys! If you think about it, it's like a french fry, so it's not *that* weird, okay? (Not as weird as my dad's peanut-butter-and-pickle sandwiches, anyway.)

Now that I'm older, while it might not sound like I'm any wiser, I actually have learned a few things, one of which is how to make perfect baked potatoes. My secret? Ditch the foil; it's your number one mistake! (Did all my Idaho friends just stand and cheer?)

Prep: 5 min *Cook:* 1 hour *Total:* 1 hour 5 min *Yield:* 5 servings

5 large russet potatoes

3 tablespoons olive oil

¼ cup flaked sea salt

Butter, sour cream, shredded cheddar cheese, and cooked and crumbled bacon for topping

1. Preheat oven to 350 degrees F. Wash and thoroughly dry each potato. Place an oven-safe cooling rack atop a rimmed baking sheet. (Baking potatoes on a rack this way allows air to circulate around the potatoes and ensures a crisp skin; it also prevents any excess oil from dripping onto the oven.) Pour oil in a shallow bowl; spread salt over a dinner plate.

2. Roll each potato in oil and then in salt, making sure to coat the entire potato evenly with both. Arrange potatoes on the cooling rack. With a sharp knife, carefully cut a zigzag pattern in the skin on top of each potato; alternatively, use the tines of a fork to pierce the skin in a zigzag pattern.

3. Bake 60 to 75 minutes, or until tender (when pierced with a fork, the tines will easily slide all the way in). Remove from the oven and serve topped with butter, sour cream, shredded cheese, and crumbled bacon.

NOTE: Read some Potato Tips on the next page.

Grayson Tip:
Always make sure you wash the potatoes first. One time I forgot and my baked potato tasted like dirt—for reals!

POTATO TIPS

- Different potatoes work better in different dishes. Red potatoes are amazing roasted and russets are best for baking and making mashed potatoes. Yukon Golds are delicious roasted, and they make great mashed potatoes, too, but they are best for making potato salad and potato soup.

- Potatoes take on a lot of water as they cook. Because of this, I recommend boiling potatoes first and then peeling them. I do this for mashed potatoes as well.

- You can tell a potato is done by piercing it all the way to the center with a steak knife or the tine of a fork. (I like to keep one by the stove whenever I make potatoes.) If the potato is fully cooked, the knife will easily slide through. A potato that is still somewhat raw will be difficult to pierce.

- Make sure you allot enough time when making a sauced potato dish or potato salad. Potatoes take longer than other starches—pasta, for example—to absorb flavor. Dressing a potato salad the day before serving it will give the flavors time to really meld together.

PEELING POTATOES

After boiling potatoes whole, wait for the potatoes to cool a little and then hold one in a towel or hot pad with one hand. With the other hand, use a paring knife to pierce the peel. Then all you have to do is pull the peel down with your fingers and it slips right off.

Practice your potato peeling skills by making the Best Potato Salad recipe on page 90.

STAY CALM

It all starts in the blue Ford Aerostar van, a story I had forgotten and the lesson Mom reminded me of over the phone one day.

I was just learning how to drive, and Dad was letting me practice as we drove to my sister's soccer tournament several hours away. The route took us through the Columbia River Gorge in the Pacific Northwest—a beautiful stretch that is also quite dangerous due to numerous turns and sudden twists as it snakes its way through the canyon. I was doing okay until I took a curve a little too fast and frantically overcorrected.

Mom recounted how Dad, cool as a cucumber, had gently but firmly grabbed the steering wheel and held it steady to bring the car back under my control. She, on the other hand, had frozen in panic, utterly terrified to feel the wheels literally lift from the road. The rocking was so bad that she'd felt certain the car was going to roll. But Dad had known exactly what to do. He hadn't panicked; he'd just taken action.

For me, the most amazing part of the story was that I couldn't remember a single detail about that day.

I hung up the phone and, as the weekend went on, the scene slowly came back to me. I could actually feel the gasp I gave and the rocking of the car. How could such a scary thing have left my mind? So I asked the family, and their response was life-changing: "Maybe because Dad stayed so calm, you were able to as well. And because he reached out and held steady, gently guiding and supporting versus barking orders or humiliating you for your mistake, you were able to let it go. You were able to continue to drive without fear of not being good enough."

I wonder how much more we could do as parents if we gently steadied instead of always being so quick to react. A child who is rocking the house might need a gentle embrace or words of encouragement, not a raised voice shouting, "What are you doing?!"

Someone might ruin dinner, but there's always cereal.

Someone might spill the entire bottle of soy sauce in the teriyaki, but there are always quesadillas.

Just gently grab the wheel and steady it with love.

White Rice

The first time I cooked rice on my own, it came out gummy. The next time, I burned it on the bottom.

Rice is one of the most universal grains out there. You can turn rice into anything—a casserole, a side dish, or even a soup. Because it's used so often and in so many ways, you'd think it would be a breeze to prepare, but instead it can be a bit tricky.

So, just in case you're out there Googling "how to cook white rice," here's the right way to do it. You got this, my friend.

Prep: 2 min *Cook:* 30 min *Total:* 32 min *Yield:* 4 servings

---

1½ cups water

Pinch salt

1 tablespoon butter

1 cup long-grain white rice

1. Bring water to a boil in a medium saucepan over medium-high heat.

2. Add salt, butter, and rice. Stir immediately and bring mixture back to a boil.

3. Cover the saucepan, reduce heat to medium-low, and cook at a simmer 18 minutes. Do not uncover until 18 minutes are up.

4. Remove the lid briefly and move pan to countertop or an unused stove burner. Replace lid and allow rice to steam another 10 minutes. Fluff with a fork and serve.

How to Reheat White Rice

Leftover rice is perfect for making fried rice (there's a recipe on our website), but what if you just want to reheat leftovers? The secret to bringing rice back to life is to add a little water (about a tablespoon to start) into the rice, then microwave it. The steam will soften the rice back to its original state.

NOTE: This rice pairs well with Bottom of the Jar Chicken (page 129) or a Smothered Chicken Burrito (page 149).

Homemade Salsa

No one realizes how little self-control they have until chips and salsa are placed on the table at a Mexican restaurant. Am I right, or am I right?

This 10-minute, restaurant-style homemade salsa recipe is fresh, flavorful, and easy to make. After you try it, you'll never buy salsa again, and you might find yourself eating it every night. Just get yourself a big bowl of salty, crispy tortilla chips and toss your self-control out the window. Oh, and bring on Taco Tuesday!

Time: 10 min *Yield:* 5 cups

6 Roma tomatoes, quartered

1 to 2 jalapeños, seeded and chopped

½ red onion, roughly chopped

Juice from 1½ limes

2 cloves garlic, sliced

1 (14.5-ounce) can fire-roasted diced tomatoes

½ teaspoon granulated sugar

½ teaspoon chili powder

½ teaspoon ground cumin

½ bunch cilantro, roughly chopped

Kosher salt, to taste

Place all ingredients in blender jar, cover with lid, and pulse until salsa is slightly chunky in texture. Serve with tortilla chips and enjoy.

NOTE: Stores well up to 1 week in the refrigerator.

Broccoli Salad

When I was dating my husband, he surprised me one night with an amazing home-cooked meal: steak, rolls, loaded baked potatoes, and broccoli with cheese sauce. "Oh no!" I thought. "He has no idea how much I hate broccoli." As I started eating, however, I was so impressed with everything else that I dug into the broccoli so I wouldn't hurt his feelings. It. Was. Delicious.

For this broccoli-starring salad, there's no need to cook the veggies first. It's just a matter of mixing in the right complementary ingredients. Every kid should learn to prepare a veggie side dish and make it their own. Why not start your kids out with this one? Don't like raisins? Skip them. Want to add hard-boiled eggs? Go for it.

Prep: 15 min *Chill:* 2 hours *Total:* 2 hours 15 min *Yield:* 10 servings

Dressing

1 cup mayonnaise

¼ cup granulated sugar

1 tablespoon apple cider vinegar

In a small bowl, whisk together all ingredients; set aside.

Salad

8 cups broccoli florets

½ cup golden raisins

½ cup Craisins

½ cup frozen peas

½ cup diced red onion

1 cup shredded Colby Jack cheese

1 cup roasted and salted sunflower seeds

8 strips applewood smoked bacon, cooked crisp and crumbled (page 21)

1. In a large bowl, toss together broccoli, raisins, Craisins, frozen peas, onion, and shredded cheese. Pour dressing over top and toss until all ingredients are well coated.
2. Cover and refrigerate at least 2 hours.
3. Just before serving, add sunflower seeds and bacon crumbles, tossing until evenly distributed.

Storing Produce

• Hang bananas to avoid browning.
• Never put tomatoes in the fridge unless they've already been sliced.
• Keep green beans stored loosely in a crisper drawer.
• Store asparagus upright in a glass with a bit of water.
• Keep broccoli chilled in a crisper drawer.
• If in doubt about how to store produce, think about how you found it when you bought it.

3-Cheese Tomato Salad

Fresh-from-the-garden juicy tomatoes marinated in a sweet, tangy balsamic dressing full of fresh herbs, lots of garlic, and, of course, 3 cheeses—now, that's a golden summer to dream of.

Prep: 10 min   *Rest:* 3 hours   *Total:* 3 hours 10 min   *Yield:* 6 to 8 servings

5 medium tomatoes (see Pro Tip)

⅓ cup olive oil

2 tablespoons balsamic vinegar

1 teaspoon granulated sugar

2 teaspoons honey

1 tablespoon freshly grated Parmesan cheese

2 small cloves garlic, minced

1 tablespoon minced fresh parsley, plus more for garnishing

1 tablespoon minced fresh basil, plus more for garnishing

Salt and pepper, to taste

1 cup crumbled feta cheese

1 cup chopped fresh mozzarella cheese

1. Slice tomatoes (each slice should be about ½-inch thick) and arrange on a lipped platter; set aside.

2. In a liquid measuring cup, combine olive oil, balsamic vinegar, sugar, honey, Parmesan cheese, garlic, parsley, basil, salt, and pepper. Whisk vigorously to emulsify oil, then pour over the tomatoes in the dish.

3. Cover platter with plastic wrap and marinate 2 to 3 hours on the countertop. If prepared more than 3 hours in advance of serving, chill in the refrigerator, but bring tomatoes to room temperature before serving.

4. Just before serving, arrange feta crumbles and fresh mozzarella on platter and sprinkle with additional chopped basil and parsley. Season with salt and pepper, to taste.

Claire Tip:
This recipe was made because Mom let us go to the farmer's market to pick out veggies. It was so fun, and the different people selling things gave out lots of samples. If you don't have a garden, go to the market; there are always people with treats there too!

Pro Tip: Tomatoes need a little special care. Because they are so water packed, you'll typically want to season them just prior to serving. The exception to this rule is if you're baking them in a pie, tart, or other savory dish that calls for fresh tomatoes. In that case, you'll want to release all of the water in the tomatoes. Salting them early will do just that. Then you can pat them dry before baking them in a tart or other dish.

Green Beans with Bacon

I grew up on green beans, but they didn't start out green; our green beans were purple! My youngest child was pretty excited to help me pick purple beans last summer at Grandma's house—so excited he was eating them raw. What is it about seeing all those colors and feeling the dirt on freshly picked food that makes it more appetizing? My kids are as picky as I was decades ago, but touching food has helped change that.

This recipe—with its perfectly cooked, crispy bacon, fragrant garlic, and butter (because butter makes everything taste better)—is super easy and the perfect side dish for dinner any night.

Prep: 15 min *Cook:* 15 min *Total:* 30 min *Yield:* 4 servings

4 quarts water, divided

3 cups ice cubes

1 pound whole green beans, ends trimmed and snapped in half (see note)

4 strips bacon

2 teaspoons butter

1 teaspoon brown sugar (optional)

2 teaspoons garlic seasoning with parsley, such as Johnny's Garlic Spread and Seasoning

1. Prepare a water bath: Fill a large bowl with 1 quart water and 3 cups ice; set aside.

2. Fill a large pot with remaining 3 quarts water and bring to a boil over high heat. Add beans and cook 4 to 5 minutes, until tender-crisp. Remove beans from boiling water with a slotted spoon or spider strainer and transfer immediately to the water bath. This stops them from cooking any further and helps them retain a bright green color and a tender-crisp feel.

3. Chop the bacon and cook in a large skillet over medium heat until crispy. Using a slotted spoon, transfer cooked bacon crumbles to a paper towel-lined bowl and set aside. Do not discard bacon fat.

4. Add butter to rendered bacon grease in skillet and melt over medium heat. Drain green beans and add to skillet, along with brown sugar, if using, and garlic spread seasoning. Stir to coat and sauté just until beans are warm, about 3 minutes. Stir in crumbled bacon and serve immediately.

NOTE: To use canned beans instead of fresh, start by cooking the bacon as outlined in step 3 and then add 2 (15-ounce) cans cut green beans, drained. Proceed as outlined above.

Trimming Veggies

Preparing ingredients so they cook properly is another important trick to learn in the kitchen.

To trim asparagus, hold a stalk in one hand and then snap off the end with your other hand. The end will break naturally where it should to eliminate the woody part. You can then line up the rest of the asparagus on a cutting board and use the trimmed stalk as a guide for where to chop off the remaining ends.

Do the same thing with green beans. The little ends snap off naturally just where they should.

Baked Beans

My grandpa won awards for his BBQ pork and baked beans, and while this is my recipe, it still makes me think of family. These rich and saucy baked beans are the perfect summer BBQ side dish. The *best* baked beans recipe has molasses, peppers, onions, and, of course, bacon. But the real secret isn't in the ingredients at all—it's in how we cook them.

Baking this dish in the oven with a little moisture allows the slow, steady heat to break down the fibrous beans and create a delicious caramelization in the sauce.

Prep: 5 min   *Cook:* 3 hours 10 min   *Total:* 3 hours 15 min   *Yield:* 6 to 8 servings

8 strips bacon

1 tablespoon vegetable oil, canola oil, or reserved bacon fat

1 large yellow onion, chopped

1 red bell pepper, chopped

¾ cup ketchup

¼ cup molasses

1 cup brown sugar

2 tablespoons yellow mustard

¼ teaspoon liquid smoke

3 (15-ounce) cans baked beans

Chopped cilantro (optional)

1. Preheat oven to 300 degrees F.
2. Chop the bacon before cooking it. Cook bacon in a skillet 2 to 3 minutes until crisp, and then remove the bacon with a slotted spoon, leaving the rendered fat in the pan for sautéing the onions and peppers. Add onions and peppers and sauté until onions are soft and translucent, about 8 minutes.
3. Transfer onions and peppers to a large Dutch oven or casserole dish. Add ketchup, molasses, brown sugar, mustard, liquid smoke, canned baked beans, and ⅔ of the bacon crumbles. Stir to combine, then sprinkle remaining bacon crumbles over top.
4. Bake, uncovered, 2½ to 3 hours, until bubbly and slightly thickened.
5. Serve topped with chopped cilantro, if desired.

Macaroni Salad

Macaroni salad is one of those classic side dishes that most people will just buy at the deli. But let's be honest, store-bought macaroni salad, more often than not, just isn't that good.

This classic macaroni salad recipe is ultra-creamy and tangy. It's guaranteed to be devoured at all your summer BBQs, parties, and potlucks.

Prep: 5 min   *Cook:* 10 min   *Chill:* 3 hours   *Total:* 3 hours 15 min   *Yield:* 10 servings

4 quarts water

2 tablespoons kosher salt

12 ounces (6 cups) dry elbow macaroni

½ (14-ounce) can sweetened condensed milk

1 cup mayonnaise

¼ cup granulated sugar

¼ cup apple cider vinegar

½ teaspoon salt, plus more to taste

¼ teaspoon fresh coarsely ground black pepper

1½ tablespoons Dijon or yellow mustard

¼ red onion, minced

½ green bell pepper, minced

½ red bell pepper, minced

1. In a large pot over medium-high heat, bring water to a boil. Stir in salt and macaroni noodles and cook until tender, 7 to 10 minutes. Drain noodles, rinse with cold water, drain again to completely remove water, and transfer to a large bowl. Chill in refrigerator while preparing dressing.

2. In a large bowl, whisk together sweetened condensed milk, mayonnaise, sugar, vinegar, salt, pepper, and mustard until smooth. Stir in onions and peppers.

3. Add cooked and cooled macaroni noodles and toss to coat. Cover bowl with plastic wrap and chill in refrigerator 3 hours. Stir briefly before serving.

The Secret to Perfect Pasta Salad

If you're making pasta to eat for dinner, you'll want it to be al dente so that it has a nice bite or chew—that's literally what al dente means. (And now you also speak Italian. I'm so proud of you; go make me some pizza.)

If you're making pasta for pasta salad, however, you'll want to do the opposite and overcook the pasta slightly. Overcooking the pasta will make it somewhat bloated so that it can't absorb all the sauce, but that simply means you'll have lots of sauce sitting in and on the noodles. Goodbye, bland pasta. Hello, flavor.

Italian Pasta Salad

I'll be honest with you: our kids totally pick out some of the ingredients in this homemade pasta salad with Italian dressing. Two of our kids love straight-up cold pepperoni. One even requested chicken nuggets, pepperoni, and carrot sticks for her birthday dinner a few years ago.

No words. I understand your disgust perfectly.

That's what makes this salad great, though: perfectly customizable for anyone's taste!

Prep: 20 min *Cook:* 10 min *Total:* 30 min *Yield:* 8 servings

4 quarts water

2 teaspoons kosher salt

1 pound rotini pasta

1 red bell pepper, chopped and divided

1 cup chopped pepperoni

1 cup chopped salami

½ cup sliced black olives

1 cup cubed mozzarella cheese

½ cup shredded Parmesan cheese

2 small Roma tomatoes, chopped

½ cup chopped red onion

Salt and pepper, to taste

Dressing

½ cup extra virgin olive oil

¼ cup white wine vinegar

1 tablespoon red bell peppers from above ingredient list, minced extra fine

2 tablespoons grated Parmesan cheese

1 tablespoon dried parsley

½ teaspoon onion powder

1 teaspoon minced garlic

2 teaspoons lemon juice

1 teaspoon dried basil

1 teaspoon dried oregano

1 teaspoon granulated sugar

1. In a large pot over medium-high heat, bring water to a boil. Stir in salt and rotini and cook until tender, 7 to 8 minutes. Drain noodles, rinse with cold water,

3 Rules for Making a Vinaigrette

1. Use a 3-to-1 ratio of oil to vinegar as a starting point, tasting as you go.

2. Pick an oil that matches the recipe. A vinaigrette for a berry salad works best with canola or vegetable oil rather than olive oil because the fruity notes in olive oil tend to compete with the distinct flavor of berries. On the other hand, olive oil pairs very well with savory salads that use veggies or have Italian or Greek flavors.

3. Always season with salt. Just because something's a liquid doesn't mean you can skip the seasonings.

Make your own vinaigrette and try it out on the 3-Cheese Tomato Salad on page 70.

drain again to completely remove water, and transfer to a large bowl. Set aside or chill in refrigerator while preparing dressing.

2. Make the dressing: To a wide-mouth mason jar, add all dressing ingredients. Secure lid and shake well; set aside.

3. Remove pasta from refrigerator and mix in remaining bell peppers, chopped pepperoni, chopped salami, sliced olives, cubed mozzarella, shredded Parmesan, tomatoes, and onions.

4. Pour dressing over pasta mixture and toss to coat. Season with salt and pepper and serve immediately.

Cheesy Potato Casserole

I grew up on scalloped potatoes, either homemade or from a box. This homemade version, with its layers upon layers of thinly sliced potatoes in a creamy cheese sauce and extra cheese on top, is still one of my absolute favorite recipes from Mom. She and I loved the potatoes along the edges of the dish because they developed the crispiest cheese topping.

The secret to a good potato casserole is to slice the potatoes thin enough that they'll cook evenly but not so thin as to make them translucent, which can lead to a mushy casserole. If assembled in the morning, this casserole can be placed in the fridge until later when you're ready to bake.

Prep: 20 min *Cook:* 2 hours *Additional:* 15 min
Total: 2 hours 35 min *Yield:* 10 to 12 servings

4 tablespoons unsalted butter

1 yellow onion, minced

8 cloves garlic, minced

¼ cup all-purpose flour

Dash ground nutmeg

1½ cups chicken broth or vegetable broth

1½ cups heavy cream (see note)

1 tablespoon salt

1 teaspoon freshly ground black pepper

1 teaspoon McCormick Montreal Chicken Seasoning

2¼ cups shredded cheddar Jack cheese, divided

2¼ cups shredded sharp cheddar cheese, divided

5 pounds russet potatoes, peeled and sliced thin (⅛ to ¼ inch)

1 cup sour cream

1 cup freshly grated Parmesan cheese, plus more for sprinkling on top

2 tablespoons freshly chopped parsley (optional)

1. Preheat oven to 400 degrees F. Spray a 3-quart baking dish with nonstick cooking spray; set aside.

2. Melt butter in a large saucepan over medium heat. Add onions and garlic and sauté 4 to 5 minutes, until tender. Sprinkle flour and nutmeg over onion mixture, then cook and stir 1 to 2 more minutes.

3. Stir in chicken broth until well combined, then add cream, salt, pepper, and Montreal seasoning. Stir until thickened, removing pan from heat just before mixture begins to boil. Off heat, stir in 1 cup shredded Jack cheese and 1 cup shredded sharp cheddar.

4. To assemble the casserole, layer ⅓ of the potato slices in prepared dish. Top with ⅓ cup sour cream by dotting small spoonfuls evenly over potatoes. Spread ⅓ of the cheese sauce over the sour cream, followed by ⅓ cup of the Parmesan cheese, ⅓ of the

Cheesy Potato Casserole *(continued)*

remaining shredded Jack cheese, and ⅓ of the remaining shredded cheddar. Repeat 2 more times, ending with the cheddar cheese and a sprinkle of Parmesan.

5. Cover pan with foil and bake 1½ to 2 hours, removing foil for the last 15 to 20 minutes, until potatoes are tender and cheese is browned.

6. Let rest 15 minutes, then top with freshly chopped parsley and serve.

NOTE: Heavy cream vs heavy whipping cream—actually, you can interchange them, they are essentially the same thing, but if you're not planning to whip it, just buy heavy cream.

Making Sauces from Scratch

I love teaching people how to make sauces—like the sauce used in this Cheesy Potato Casserole—because they're actually really simple. Start by sautéing your aromatics (also known as onions, carrots, garlic, and/or celery) in a pan to release their sugars and break down the fibers so they'll flavor the sauce without making it chunky.

Sprinkle flour or cornstarch over the sautéed veggies so the sauce will thicken nicely. Let the flour cook at least 30 to 60 seconds to cook out its flavor. (No one wants to taste flour or cornstarch in their sauce.) Next, whisk in your liquid and cook until it bubbles lightly and thickens. Stir in your cheese, whisk until it's melted, and—voila—you have a decadent cheese sauce ready to pour over potatoes or pasta.

Mashed Potatoes

IMPORTANT: BEFORE YOU START THIS RECIPE, READ THE TIPS IN THE SIDEBAR!

Growing up, I was *obsessed* with creamy mashed potatoes and roasted chicken. I used to stand next to my mom in the kitchen and peel potatoes on Sunday morning. It was such a simple routine that I'm not sure why it always stands out to me so much. Maybe that's how it is with life and memories: it's not the big stuff that comes back to you, it's just the moments when you're side by side.

These homemade mashed potatoes are rich and creamy, and will totally blow your mind. Serve alongside Slow Cooker Pot Roast (page 153).

Prep: 5 min *Cook:* 30 min *Additional:* 10 min *Total:* 45 min *Yield:* 4 to 6 servings

2 pounds russet potatoes (about 6 to 7 medium potatoes)

1 cup heavy cream, half and half, or whole milk

8 tablespoons butter, melted

1½ teaspoons salt, or to taste

Freshly ground black pepper, to taste

2 tablespoons butter, sliced into 2 pats

1. Place unpeeled potatoes in a large pot and cover with cold water.
2. Bring to a boil over medium-high heat and cook until easily pierced with a knife, about 20 to 25 minutes. Drain potatoes well and let them cool 3 to 5 minutes.
3. While potatoes cool, pour cream, half and half, or milk in a glass bowl and microwave on high power 1 to 2 minutes, until hot and steamy; set aside.
4. Once potatoes are cool enough to handle, pierce the skins on one end with a paring knife, and then grab the peels and simply slide them off.
5. Use a potato ricer to mash potatoes into a large bowl. Alternatively, roughly chop potatoes, put them in a mesh strainer, and push them through the strainer with a curved wooden spoon.
6. Using a wooden spoon or rubber spatula, stir the melted

Tips for Making the Best Mashed Potatoes

• Use a potato ricer. Starchy potatoes need to be lightened up a bit; otherwise, they can become gooey and sticky when whipped into mashed potatoes. Using a ricer instead of a mixer adds air to the potatoes and removes excess water. If you don't have a ricer, you can press the potatoes through a fine mesh sieve to get the same effect. Just remember: more air = fluffier potatoes.

• Never add milk or cream to potatoes until after you've stirred in the butter. Milk products contain water that can combine with the starches in the potatoes and turn them to glue. Adding the butter first coats the potatoes in a protective layer of fat, which results in silkier potatoes.

butter into the potatoes. Test the temperature of the cream and heat for another 30 seconds if needed. Add the hot cream and salt and pepper and stir again until smooth.

7. Top bowl of potatoes with 2 pats butter and serve immediately.

Peyton Tip:
Wait for the potatoes to cool a little and then hold them in a towel or hot pad in one hand and a little knife in the other to pierce the peel. Then all you have to do is pull the peel down and it comes right off.

Try serving these up with a little grated cheese and cooked bacon on top! It's so good!

Tex-Mex Salad

I discovered the pandemic lockdown in 2020 was the perfect time to get the kids in the kitchen to teach them not just how to cook but, through cooking, about a lot of other things, too. Trust me on this, side-by-side cooking with your loved ones will *change your family.* You will find no greater joy than allowing hearts to connect, and it's not by chance that food becomes the central force in bringing people together.

Kids can easily tear lettuce as toddlers, stir dressing as small children, slice and dice as tweens, and cook the meat as teens. This salad is the perfect recipe for all ages. Bring on the perfectly cooked ground beef—come learn how to not dry it out.

Prep: 20 min   *Cook:* 8 min   *Total:* 28 min   *Yield:* 8 servings

For the Meat

1 pound ground beef

1 tablespoon taco seasoning

½ cup water

For the Salad

1 heart romaine lettuce, rinsed and chopped

1 (15-ounce) can black beans, rinsed and drained

2 green bell peppers, diced

1 jalapeño pepper, seeded and diced (see note)

4 small tomatoes, chopped

1 red onion, diced

1 cup frozen roasted corn (see note)

1 handful cilantro leaves, chopped

1 to 2 avocados, chopped

1 cup cubed Colby Jack, Monterey Jack, or pepper jack cheese

2 cups crushed tortilla chips or Doritos chips

1 recipe Ranch-Tomatillo Dressing (see recipe below)

1. In a large skillet over medium heat, cook ground beef, stirring and breaking it up with a wooden spoon, until almost no pink remains, about 8 minutes. Drain grease and

Mix Up Your Salad

Salads are very versatile and can take on many different flavors, colors, and textures. Try one—or more—of these ideas next time you make a salad:

- Use different-sized ingredients
- Use something sweet
- Use something savory
- Use something salty

Using a variety of ingredients results in a fulfilling meal that will make both your body and mind happy. It's the secret to a really good salad.

Mix up your own flavors with this salad or the Broccoli Salad on page 69.

Tex-Mex Salad *(continued)*

Peyton Tip:

All of us kids started out really picky. My mom says that's because she was once picky. I'm the least picky, Claire is getting way better, and Grayson is, well, let's just say it takes a lot of coaxing. This salad is awesome because Mom lets me use these two big salsa-and-chip platters to arrange each ingredient, and then we can all build our own salad. That way Grayson can skip the corn and take extra cheese and I can load up on all of it.

return the skillet to the stovetop. Stir in taco seasoning and water and cook until slightly thickened and all meat is coated in sauce, about 2 minutes. Remove from heat and set aside.

2. In a large bowl, toss together lettuce, beans, peppers, tomatoes, onions, corn, cilantro, avocado, cubed cheese, and chips. Add beef and toss to combine.

3. Pour dressing over top a little at a time and toss until coated to your taste. Serve remaining dressing on the side.

NOTE: For a spicier salad, slice the jalapeño and leave the seeds intact.

NOTE: We prefer to use frozen roasted corn, which is sometimes called Mexican street corn. If you can't find frozen roasted corn, regular frozen corn will work as well.

Ranch-Tomatillo Dressing

1 cup prepared ranch dressing

1 tomatillo, husk removed and halved

½ teaspoon lime juice

2 tablespoons taco seasoning

Handful fresh cilantro leaves

Add all ingredients to the jar of a blender and process until smooth. Store in an airtight container in the refrigerator up to 1 week.

The Best Potato Salad

Before you read anything, and I'll remind you a million more times, start this potato salad THE DAY BEFORE you intend to eat it.

The best potato salad in the entire United States of America has arrived. Forget your mom and grandma's potato salad recipe when you need to bring a BBQ side dish. I've tested potato salads for years now, and I can tell you, this is the only recipe you need.

Prep: 30 min *Cook:* 10 min *Chill:* 8 hours *Total:* 8 hours 40 min *Yield:* 10 servings

5 pounds Yukon Gold potatoes

2 cups mayonnaise

2½ teaspoons yellow mustard

1 tablespoon Dijon mustard

1 tablespoon apple cider vinegar

1 tablespoon chopped fresh dill

¼ to ½ teaspoon celery salt

½ teaspoon smoked paprika, plus some for garnish

¾ cup sweet relish

2 baby pickles, sweet or dill, chopped

2 green onions, chopped

10 hard-boiled eggs, peeled and chopped

½ teaspoon salt, or more, to taste

1. At least 8 to 9 hours before serving, roughly chop potatoes (skins on), then add to a large pot and cover with water. Bring to a boil over medium-high heat and cook until tender when pricked with the tines of a fork, about 10 to 15 minutes.
2. While potatoes cook, prepare dressing. In a medium bowl, stir together mayonnaise, mustards, vinegar, dill, celery salt, paprika, relish, pickles, and green onions; set aside.
3. Drain water off potatoes and let them cool 4 to 5 minutes. Once cool enough to handle, use a paring knife to remove skins. Transfer ¾ of the potatoes to a large bowl. Pour dressing over potatoes and gently fold to combine.
4. Peel and mince remaining potatoes and fold into the salad, along with chopped eggs. Season with salt, to taste.
5. Sprinkle a little paprika over the top, cover with plastic wrap, and chill at least 8 hours, or overnight.

NOTE: You can boil whole potatoes, place in a bowl and cover tightly in plastic wrap, then store them for up to 2 days in the fridge.

Fettuccine Alfredo P. 102

PASTA
& PIZZA

Cheesy Pesto Pasta

Need dinner on the table in 20 minutes? This recipe fits the bill. It tastes fresh but uses ingredients you probably already have on hand. It's also a great special-diets recipe because there isn't any meat involved, and you can easily use gluten-free pasta.

Prep: 5 min   *Cook:* 10 min   *Additional:* 15 min (for Pesto)
Total: 15 to 30 min   *Yield:* 4 servings

4 quarts water

2 teaspoons salt

1 pound angel hair pasta (see note)

½ teaspoon extra virgin olive oil

1 clove garlic, minced

2 cups halved grape tomatoes

1 cup shredded mozzarella cheese

Fresh ground black pepper, for serving

Pesto

5½ tablespoons pine nuts

3 cloves garlic, unpeeled

3 cups packed fresh basil leaves

5 to 6 tablespoons olive oil

6 tablespoons grated Parmesan cheese

Salt, to taste

1. In a large pot over high heat, bring water to a boil. Add salt and pasta. Cook until al dente, according to package directions.

2. Meanwhile, make pesto (see note): Heat a large skillet over medium heat. When skillet is hot, add pine nuts and garlic. Toast 2 to 3 minutes, occasionally shaking the pan or using a wooden spoon to toss the pine nuts. When pine nuts are a nice golden brown, transfer to a bowl but return garlic to the pan so it can continue roasting about 2 minutes, or until brown is starting to show through. Peel skins from garlic and discard. Let garlic cool to room temperature.

3. Place toasted pine nuts, roasted garlic, basil, and 5 tablespoons olive oil to the jar of a blender and pulse until pureed. It should still be a tad grainy in texture. If it seems too grainy, add up to 1 tablespoon more olive oil and process again.

Tips for Cooking Pasta

- Your pot should be taller than your pasta, meaning you need to stop overcrowding the noodles in that saucepan and buy a big pot.

- Always heavily salt the water. Seriously, salt it until it tastes like seawater. Add salt, stir, and then taste the water. I won't tell anyone if you use your finger as long as you wash before and after.

- Never add pasta until the water is boiling. Pasta will break down as soon as you add it, so it will become mushy if the water isn't crazy hot.

- To prevent pasta from sticking, hot water is key, but you should also always stir to separate the noodles as soon as they sink into the pot.

4. Transfer mixture to a small bowl and stir in Parmesan cheese. Taste and season with salt as needed. Serve immediately or refrigerate in an airtight container. Drizzle a thin layer of olive oil over pesto, seal lid, and store in the refrigerator up to 3 weeks. Just make sure you continually refresh the layer of olive oil. As long as the pesto is covered with oil, it will stay fresh and green.

5. When pasta is almost al dente, heat oil in a large skillet over medium heat. When oil shimmers, stir in garlic and sauté 20 seconds, until fragrant. Reduce heat to medium-low.

6. Quickly drain pasta and add to skillet, along with the pesto and grape tomatoes. Use tongs to toss noodles until coated with pesto. Add cheese and toss again.

7. Serve immediately topped with a few cracks fresh ground pepper.

NOTE: Gluten-free pasta or zucchini noodles can be used in place of pasta.

NOTE: You can make fresh pesto in the summer, then freeze it in an ice cube tray. Once frozen, release cubes from the tray, transfer to freezer bags, and store for months in the freezer.

RECIPE SUBSTITUTIONS

Sometimes you have to substitute ingredients. Life happens, and you end up with a missing this or that. Luckily, there are lots of clever shortcuts and substitutes to keep you moving forward.

When substituting ingredients, look for what's similar. No tomato sauce? Try pureeing your fresh tomatoes or adding water to tomato paste.

Using a processed ingredient versus fresh generally means the flavor will be more salty and less, well, fresh. Balance that by holding back on seasoning until the new ingredient has cooked in, and try to find something to brighten things up, even if it's just a little parsley.

Similar textures or flavors can be used as well. For example, looking to make your soup vegetarian? Ground beef can be skipped and beans and roasted sweet potatoes used to still give a filling feeling.

Remember, substituting means you need to change expectations. Things will not turn out exactly the same, so always try to stick strictly to a recipe the first time you try it.

Here are a few suggestions, but Google is your bestie if you need more ideas.

- SOUR CREAM: equal amounts of yogurt, mayonnaise, applesauce, or mashed bananas
- 1 CUP BUTTERMILK: 1 cup milk with 1 tablespoon vinegar or lemon juice
- GROUND BEEF: any ground meat or beans
- MILK: nondairy milk is fine in most recipes
- HEAVY CREAM (other than for whipping): half and half or milk
- 1 TEASPOON BAKING POWDER: ¼ teaspoon baking soda plus ½ teaspoon cream of tartar
- 1 TEASPOON BAKING SODA: 4 teaspoons baking powder
- ALCOHOL: a matching color juice or stock. For example, white wine = chicken broth or white apple or grape juice. Red wine = grape juice or diluted balsamic vinegar.
- 1 CUP BREAD FLOUR: 1 cup all-purpose flour
- 1 CUP CAKE FLOUR: 1 cup all-purpose flour minus 2 tablespoons; sift remaining flour with 2 tablespoons cornstarch
- 1 CUP SELF-RISING FLOUR: ⅞ cup all-purpose flour plus 1½ teaspoons baking powder and ½ teaspoon salt
- 1 CLOVE GARLIC: ½ teaspoon garlic powder
- 1 LARGE EGG FOR BAKING: ¼ cup carbonated water or 2 tablespoons water plus 2 teaspoons baking powder plus 1 teaspoon vegetable oil

The Best Macaroni and Cheese

Is putting hot dogs in macaroni and cheese still a thing? (I hope not.) This ultra-creamy dish is loaded with three different kinds of cheese and pretty much everything you could ever want out of homemade mac and cheese. Say "Sayonara" to the standard blue box version and say "Hello" to your new favorite recipe. No hot dogs required.

Prep: 45 min   *Cook:* 10 min   *Total:* 55 min   *Yield:* 12 servings

Mac and Cheese

¼ cup cornstarch

2 cups shredded Monterey Jack cheese

4 cups shredded sharp cheddar cheese

2 tablespoons kosher salt

1 (16-ounce) package elbow macaroni noodles

4 tablespoons butter, cubed

¼ cup minced yellow onion

1 teaspoon ground mustard

3 cups whole milk

2 cups heavy cream

1 teaspoon Worcestershire sauce

¼ teaspoon hot sauce (optional)

½ teaspoon salt

½ teaspoon pepper

Topping

4 slices bread, torn into pieces

2 tablespoons butter, cubed

½ cup shredded Parmesan cheese

½ teaspoon salt

½ teaspoon pepper

1. Preheat oven to 400 degrees F. and butter a 9x13-inch casserole dish..

2. In a large bowl, toss together the cornstarch and cheeses. Set aside.

3. In a large pot of boiling water, add kosher salt and pasta. Cook until just past al dente. Drain and set aside.

4. In a large pot over medium heat, add butter. Once melted, add onion and cook for 2 to 3 minutes or until tender. Add the mustard, milk, and cream and bring to a simmer.

5. Add cornstarch-and-cheese mixture, whisking until smooth. Add Worcestershire and hot sauce, if desired, and salt and pepper to taste.

6. Add cooked pasta to the pot, heat for 2 minutes, then pour mixture into prepared casserole dish.

7. To make the topping: Pulse the bread, butter, Parmesan, salt, and pepper in a food processor until coarsely ground. Sprinkle bread crumbs over pasta.

8. Bake 10 minutes or until golden brown.

Pan-Fried Tortellini

Cade introduced me to cheesy pan-fried tortellini when we first got married. I had never eaten tortellini before, but I quickly loved it, and I set out to learn how to make it. We both had a lot to learn back then, and this recipe was perfect to play around with.

Pan-Fried Tortellini is one of our favorite dinners both because of how easy it is and because you can add whatever veggies or even meats you have on hand, and it's always delicious.

Prep: 10 min   *Cook:* 20 min   *Total:* 30 min   *Yield:* 4 to 6 servings

2 to 3 tablespoons olive oil, divided

2 cloves garlic, minced

1 large carrot, peeled and sliced thin

1 cup julienned sweet red peppers or bell peppers

½ cup sliced mushrooms

½ cup oil-packed sun-dried tomatoes

1 (16-ounce) carton fresh tortellini (see note)

1 cup frozen peas, thawed

2 cups shredded mozzarella cheese

Salt and pepper, to taste

1. Heat 1 tablespoon oil in a large skillet over medium-high heat until oil begins to shimmer. Add garlic and stir until fragrant, 30 to 60 seconds. Add the carrots and cook until tender, about 4 minutes. Add the peppers and mushrooms and sauté an additional 3 minutes or until tender. Set aside.

2. Cook tortellini according to package directions, drain in a colander over the sink, and set aside.

3. Add 1 to 2 tablespoons sun-dried tomato oil to the pan and let it heat until it shimmers. Stir in cooked tortellini and sun-dried tomatoes and sauté until the tortellini begins to brown and the flavors combine, about 3 minutes.

4. Stir in sautéed vegetables, peas, mozzarella, and salt and pepper. Serve immediately.

NOTE: We love the fresh tortellini versus the dried. Find it in the refrigerated section.

Pro Tip: Have your kids help you choose the mix-ins for this dish. Claire once threw in chopped-up pepperoni (surprise, surprise), and the dish tasted like pizza tortellini. Here are some of our favorite options.

- Artichoke hearts
- Asparagus
- Carrots
- Mushrooms
- Olives
- Peppers
- Snap peas
- Tomatoes (cherry or grape tomatoes are best for this recipe)
- Yellow squash
- Zucchini

Fettuccine Alfredo

My dad traveled a lot when I was a kid. One night, after returning home from a long business trip, he immediately left to attend a meeting at a local Italian restaurant, and because Mom felt strongly about the importance of having family dinner together, she hauled all five of us kids there too. Mom probably had her hands full keeping us quiet in a restaurant. But she was determined to make sure we were all together for dinner whenever—and wherever—we could be.

Prep: 15 min   *Cook:* 25 min   *Total:* 40 min   *Yield:* 6 to 8 servings

4 to 6 quarts water

¼ cup kosher salt

16 ounces fettuccine

6 tablespoons unsalted butter

2 garlic cloves, minced

½ teaspoon Dijon mustard

2 tablespoons cream cheese

1 cup heavy cream

½ cup milk

½ cup grated Parmigiano-Reggiano

1¼ cups grated Parmesan cheese, divided

½ teaspoon salt

¼ teaspoon ground black pepper

1 teaspoon lemon juice

1 tablespoon fresh minced parsley, for garnishing

Fresh ground pepper, for garnishing

1. In a large pot over medium-high heat, combine water and kosher salt. Bring to a boil.
2. While water comes to a boil, melt butter in a high-sided skillet or large Dutch oven over medium heat. Add garlic and mustard and stir until fragrant, 30 seconds to 1 minute.
3. Whisk in cream cheese until smooth and melted, then quickly whisk in heavy cream and milk. Bring to a simmer, stirring occasionally.
4. Stir in Parmigiano-Reggiano and ½ cup Parmesan cheese. Cook sauce 10 minutes, or until thickened. Salt and pepper to taste.
5. Add fettucine to boiling water, and cook until al dente, 8 to 13 minutes.
6. Whisk lemon juice into the sauce (this will balance the acidity).
7. Using tongs, remove cooked fettuccine from water and transfer to sauce, along with ½ cup Parmesan cheese. Stir with tongs to combine.
8. Serve immediately, topped with remaining Parmesan cheese, fresh parsley, and fresh ground pepper.

NOTE: This recipe tastes great with grilled chicken or our Perfect Chicken in a Pan (page 121). Slice the chicken into thin strips and mix it into sauce when adding the noodles.

Pasta Bolognese

I once took a cooking class in Italy. The food ended up being really yummy, but the instruction was horrible. The chef never let the class join in until the very end for some quick pasta making. Learning happens with your ears, eyes, hands, and mouth. You need to see it, feel it, taste it. It's the only way.

I was pretty disappointed in the class and the chef, but then he taught us the secret to authentic Italian Bolognese sauce and had us try it. What was the secret? Bolognese needs lemon juice: it's bright and acidic and breaks up the monotony of tomatoes, adding another layer to a perfect sauce.

Prep: 35 min   *Cook:* 3 hours   *Total:* 3 hours 35 min   *Yield:* 8 to 10 servings

---

2 carrots

2 stalks celery

1 red onion

6 cloves garlic

2 cups halved Roma tomatoes

1 tablespoon olive oil, plus more for roasting tomatoes

1 tablespoon butter

1 pound 80-percent lean ground beef

1 pound ground Italian sausage

2 (15-ounce) cans tomato sauce

1 (15-ounce) can fire-roasted diced tomatoes

¼ cup heavy cream (see note)

¼ cup milk

1 teaspoon white cooking wine (see note)

Zest of 1 lemon

1 squeeze of lemon juice

Dash ground nutmeg

2 bay leaves

Salt and pepper, to taste

1 (16-ounce) package pasta, cooked according to package directions

Freshly grated Parmesan cheese, for serving

1. Preheat oven to 425 degrees F.
2. Mince carrots, celery, onion, garlic. Set aside.
3. Spread tomatoes on rimmed baking sheet and drizzle with olive oil and salt, to taste. Roast 20 minutes, until tomatoes are soft and charred in several places. Remove from oven and cool 5 minutes. Transfer roasted tomatoes to the jar of a blender and process to make a slightly chunky sauce. Set aside.
4. Heat 1 tablespoon olive oil and 1 tablespoon butter in a Dutch oven over medium heat until butter melts. Add carrots, celery, and onion

Grayson Tip:
I love to take pieces of sandwich bread, butter them, sprinkle on garlic seasoning, and then put them under the broiler to go with our meal. You don't even have to buy special bread.

Herbs and Spices

Fresh vs Dry Herbs

Fresh herbs are obviously my fave, but I can't get them all year, so I remember this simple rule: To use dried herbs instead of fresh herbs, use *half* the amount. For instance, 1 teaspoon of fresh basil is ½ teaspoon dry.

Blooming Spices

The real secret to making a great sauce is blooming the spices. That's when you place spices directly in the hot pan and the heat brings out the extra flavor. Any recipe that calls for spices—think soups, sauces, and seasoning on meat—can use this technique.

and sauté, stirring occasionally, until tender, about 5 minutes. Add garlic and cook 1 minute.

5. Add ground beef and sausage, breaking it up into very small pieces with a wooden spoon or a plastic meat chopper (which is our preferred method), and cook until meat is cooked through, about 10 minutes. Drain off excess grease.

6. Return to heat and stir in blended tomatoes, canned tomato sauce, diced tomatoes, cream, milk, white wine, lemon zest, 1 squirt lemon juice, nutmeg, and bay leaves. Stir to combine, taste, and add salt and pepper as desired.

7. Bring to a simmer over medium heat. Continue to simmer at least 2 to 3 hours or up to 5 hours.

8. Discard bay leaves and serve over cooked pasta. Garnish generously with freshly grated Parmesan cheese.

NOTE: You can substitute the ¼ cup cream and ¼ cup milk for ½ cup whole milk, if desired, but do not use a low-fat milk if not also using heavy cream.

NOTE: If using white wine instead of white cooking wine, use 2 teaspoons.

FOUR ELEMENTS OF COOKING

So, are you ready to learn the most important thing ever about cooking? It's this: there are four magical elements that, when combined, turn out a perfect dinner every time.

Salt, fat, acid, heat. Mastering these four elements in your cooking is the true secret to success. They're so important, in fact, that the famed chef and food writer Samin Nosrat wrote an entire book about them and also stars in a Netflix documentary series centered on them.

Salt. Salt highlights the sweet and can even make an ingredient taste more like itself by subtly enhancing it. Salt also balances flavors and can make something that tastes bland suddenly taste awesome. A recipe that comes out tasting bland is almost always one that didn't call for enough salt.

Fat. Butter, oil, marbling in meat—they all add flavor to a dish. I love what Nosrat says in the first episode of her popular Netflix series: "Fat adds its own unique flavor to a dish, and it can amplify the other flavors in a recipe. Simply put, fat makes food delicious—and one of the most important things any cook can learn is how to harness its magic."

Acid. I will never forget being with the winner of the show *Top Chef* while participating in a cooking competition in California. I was making a creamy sauce for our Panko-Crusted Chicken with Lemon Cream Sauce (you can find the recipe on our blog, ohsweetbasil.com) when he walked over and said, "Never add the lemon juice until the end; and, good for you, acid is one of the keys to cooking, especially in a sauce." I immediately changed my recipe to add the lemon at the very end of the recipe and have held on to that tip. Acid breaks up and adds contrast to a dish as well as punches up the flavor to a new level.

Heat. Not only does heat cook your food, but it is also the element that transforms it. You can bake a chicken breast, but to brown it in a pan with a little butter, salt, and pepper, and a squeeze of lemon at the end? Now we are talking. Heat brings out the natural sugars in a food and works to caramelize meat, veggies, and even fruits. Heat is the master, and it's important to learn how different levels of heat—high or low, fast or slow—can make or break a perfect dish.

PIZZA, PIZZA!

SECRETS TO ARTISAN PIZZA

Before baking pizza dough, always place a pizza stone or pizza steel (links for recommended products can be found at ohsweetbasil.com/shop) in the oven and heat the oven to 550 degrees F. or to the highest temperature your oven will allow. The pizza stone needs to heat at this temperature for 45 minutes in order to be sufficiently hot to cook the crust of the pizza. If you do not have a baking stone, you can turn a cookie sheet upside down and heat it in the oven for 10 to 20 minutes.

A pizza peel is a must to help you move the pizza into the oven and onto the hot pizza stone to bake. Flour the peel and place the dough on, then add toppings. Slide the peel all the way into the oven, touching the back of the pizza stone or pan with the lip of the peel, and give little jerks back toward you to slide the dough off the peel.

A NOTE ABOUT FLOUR

00 flour, a special type of extra-fine Italian milled flour, is similar to all-purpose flour but with a different protein content.

Basically, 00's muscles are a little bit different from all-purpose's muscles. And, while both are awesome, 00's muscles are perfect for pizza.

PEPPERONI

The secret to perfect pepperoni as a topping is easy. Layer pepperoni between two paper towels. Place on a plate, and microwave on high power 5 to 7 seconds. That will remove some of the grease and dry out the meat so you get those crisp edges.

CHEESE

Not all shredded mozzarella is created equal. Pre-grated cheese is packaged with preservatives to keep it fresh, and those same preservatives tend to change the flavor and texture of melted cheese. When you grate cheese yourself, it will taste fresher and melt more easily. I recommend using a low-moisture whole milk cheese.

If you're looking to make your margherita pizza special, buy buffalo mozzarella, which is usually water packed. Dry it in paper towels and then slice it into pieces to top your pizza.

A PIZZA TO REMEMBER

The reason our blog—and its name, Oh, Sweet Basil—exists is because of a pizza. One pizza was more influential in my life than I ever would have guessed. Isn't this true of life? There you are, living your life, going about the same old things, and, out of nowhere, one thing or one person changes absolutely everything.

We were eating at the Steps of Rome in California, and the margherita pizza was absolutely delicious. I just could not stop thinking about how fresh and good the ingredients were. When we got home, I felt this absolute urgency and laserlike focus on cooking. I wanted to learn more, do more, and share more, all in my kitchen.

Fast-forward a number of years to when Cade and I took a trip to Italy. On the last day of the trip, we decided to rest at our hotel in Venice and just enjoy the pool, the sights, and the moments.

Late in the afternoon, we were sitting in the lobby when a very kind staff member asked about our trip. We talked for a while, and somehow it slipped that we had yet to have an incredible pizza. I mean, pizza was what had inspired and shaped our lives with the blog, and there we were in Italy feeling kind of let down.

The young man smiled a knowing smile and told us to wait.

A few minutes later, he brought back the most perfect margherita and pepperoni pizzas I've ever seen.

Magic was happening!

The crust was so crisp and chewy, it gave me goose bumps. Who gets goose bumps over pizza? It was, hands down, to this day, the best pizza I've ever had.

I felt like all my dreams had been fulfilled. But there was more to come. . . .

The chef sauntered over and invited us into his kitchen for a private pizza lesson.

I will never forget that moment: the feel of the floured counter, the heat from those huge ovens, and the thick Italian accents and words of a few pizzaiolos (cool name for pizza makers, right?) throwing around dough like nobody's business. The chef was from Florence. He was legit.

And then he gave us his recipe. And in this book, I'm giving it to you.

Pizza Sauce

We love this recipe for homemade pizza sauce because if we're in a hurry, it takes only five minutes to make. If we have more time, though, we let it simmer for a couple of hours so the flavor just gets better and better. Seriously, if you have time, let it simmer. Oh my goodness, the smell is intoxicating.

Let's be honest, I just want to dunk cheesy carbs in this all day long, so let's not even talk about it, let's get cooking.

Prep: 15 min   *Cook:* 1 hour   *Total:* 1 hour 15 minutes   *Yield:* 24 ounces

2 teaspoons extra virgin olive oil

1 tablespoon butter

4 garlic cloves, minced

1¾ teaspoons onion powder

¼ to ½ teaspoon red pepper flakes

1½ teaspoons chopped fresh basil (or ¾ teaspoon dried)

1 teaspoon chopped fresh oregano (or ½ teaspoon dried)

5 tablespoons freshly grated Parmesan cheese

2 teaspoons brown sugar

2 (8-ounce) cans tomato sauce

4 tablespoons tomato paste

⅔ cup warm water

Salt and pepper, to taste

1. Heat oil and butter in a large pot over medium heat until almost shimmering. Add garlic and stir briefly. Quickly add onion powder, red pepper flakes, basil, and oregano. Stir briefly to allow the herbs to bloom.
2. Stir in Parmesan cheese and brown sugar, followed quickly by tomato sauce, tomato paste, and water.
3. Bring sauce to a simmer, reduce heat to low, and season with salt and pepper, to taste. Sauce can be served immediately but will develop a deeper, richer flavor if simmered 1 to 2 hours.

NOTE: Sauce can be cooled and stored in a sealed jar in the refrigerator for up to 3 weeks, or in the freezer for up to 3 months.

Peyton Tip:
Pizza sauce is actually how I learned all about fresh herbs, which totally make a difference in this recipe. But the real secret tip to this recipe is a cooking term Mom taught me called, blooming the spices. Look on page 106 to learn about herbs, spices, and blooming spices.

Pizza Dough

I love to use this pizza dough recipe to teach others about the patience of fermentation. (See pages 36–37 for a quick lesson about yeast.) Those gas bubbles from the carbon dioxide in the pizza crust make it chewier. With other yeast doughs, we don't want bubbles (think sandwich bread and dinner rolls), so we don't let the dough rise for hours and hours. Fermentation is key in pizza dough, so try to give your yeast at least the day to ferment.

I've altered this classic recipe slightly so you can still get a perfect Italian pizza without spending 48 hours waiting. And when you make it, I hope you laugh, talk with poorly attempted Italian accents, and enjoy the heck out of your pizza.

Prep: 30 min   *Rest:* 24 hours   *Cook:* 10 min
Total: 24 hours 40 min   *Yield:* 2 (10-inch) pizzas

1½ cups (350 grams) warm (100 degrees F.) water

2 teaspoons (10 grams) fine sea salt

1 pinch granulated sugar

¼ teaspoon (1.5 grams) instant yeast

4 cups (500 grams) white flour, such as 00 flour (Italian milled flour) or baker's flour (see page 108)

The Day Before Baking

1. At least 1 day before assembling pizza, stir together warm water and salt in a large liquid measuring cup. Add sugar and yeast and stir to combine. Let rest a few minutes, until foamy.

2. In a large bowl, use clean hands to combine flour and water-yeast mixture until a slightly sticky dough forms. Once dough is formed, let it rest 30 seconds and then knead it in the bowl with your hands for 1 minute. Set bowl aside, uncovered, and rest 20 to 30 minutes.

3. Turn out dough onto lightly floured surface and knead 30 to 45 seconds, until dough is relaxed and smooth. Lightly oil a clean bowl and add the dough, turning once, so the seam is on the bottom. Cover tightly with a lid or plastic wrap and let dough rise 1½ to 2 hours. If your house is cold, heat oven to 250 degrees F., turn off oven, open oven door, and place the dough bowl on the door.

4. When dough has risen, carefully turn the bowl on its side and use your hand to help the dough fall gently to a lightly floured counter. (Do not grab and lift the dough, as this will stretch it too much.) Divide dough into 2 pieces and shape each piece into a ball. Place each shaped piece on a floured board or baking sheet, dust the tops with flour, and cover tightly with plastic wrap. Let dough rest overnight. Once dough has finished this third rest, you can use it immediately or store it on a pan in the refrigerator up to 1 day. Let chilled dough come to room temperature before stretching.

Pizza Dough *(continued)*

The Day You Bake

5. Forty-five minutes before assembling pizza, place a pizza stone or cast-iron pizza pan on the center rack of the oven and heat oven to 550 degrees F. (A very hot pizza stone helps the crust cook quickly, which means the cheese topping won't burn before the crust is crisp and finished.) If your oven doesn't go this high, set it to the highest temperature possible. Then, 10 minutes before baking pizza, set broiler to high.

6. Flour a pizza peel so it will be ready to hold the crust as soon as it is shaped. To shape crust, place dough ball on a floured surface and use your fingertips to tap the top around the outer edges and establish the base shape of the crust. (Tap your fingers like they are pouncing quickly on the dough.) This will form an edge or lip around the crust. Once you have your shape, gently pick up the dough and hold it like you would a steering wheel, leaving your thumbs under the lip of the crust so you don't press it thin. Start turning the pizza like you would a steering wheel, allowing the dough to hang down and brush the countertop as you rotate it. Carefully work it into a 10-inch circle, occasionally using a closed fist to reshape it in the center. Stretching the dough this way, as opposed to rolling it out, keeps the dough from becoming tough and dense. Once the crust is formed, place it on the prepared peel and top as desired.

7. If your broiler is still set to high, turn it off, then set your oven to the highest temperature allowed before placing the pizza in the oven.

8. Lift the peel and hold it in the oven directly above your pizza stone or pan. The front tip of the peel should be above the back edge of your pizza pan. Gently jiggle the pizza peel back and forth as you pull it toward you and bring it out of the oven so the dough comes off the peel and onto the pan. Bake until edges are golden brown, about 10 minutes.

Tips for Making Pizza Dough

- Use a thermometer to test the temperature of the water before you proof your yeast. It matters, and it's just a simple task.
- Use your hands. No mixers, please. (If you want to do it like an Italian, you have to use your hands.)
- Weigh your ingredients. Invest in a kitchen scale that allows you to zero out the scale after putting the bowl on so each ingredient is measured correctly.

Traditional Italian Pepperoni Pizza

When I was little, sometimes we would go visit my older sister at her job at Sunshine Pizza. There was a little arcade room (hello, '90s!), and I'm positive the phone was hanging on a wall and some teenager was taking an order while twisting her finger through the spiraled cord.

I hated pizza. All that red sauce and weird toppings like mushrooms, gag. But sixth grade changed that. As the top dogs of the school, we got to eat lunch in our classroom. Every Friday we would pool our money to split a delivery order of pizza.

Years later, I just had to dive in and discover everything about LEGIT homemade pizza. Like, guys, you might not ever get takeout again.

Prep: 24 hours 35 min (if preparing dough and sauce from scratch)
Cook: 10 min *Total:* 24 hours 45 min

Prep: 45 min (if using prepared dough and sauce)
Cook: 10 min *Total:* 55 min *Yield:* 1 (8-inch) pizza

---

1 recipe prepared Pizza Dough
    (page 113)

⅓ to ¾ cup bottled or homemade Pizza
    Sauce (page 110)

6 ounces Boar's Head sliced pepperoni
    (in the deli section)

3 to 4 cups shredded low-moisture
    whole milk mozzarella cheese

Pizza stone (see page 108)

Pizza peel

1. Forty-five minutes before assembling pizza, place a pizza stone or cast-iron pizza pan on the center rack of the oven and heat oven to 550 degrees F. (A very hot pizza stone helps the crust cook quickly, which means the cheese topping won't burn before the crust is crisp and finished.) If your oven doesn't go this high, set it to the highest temperature possible. Then, 10 minutes before baking pizza, set broiler to high.

2. Flour a pizza peel so it will be ready to hold the crust as soon as it is shaped. To shape crust, place dough ball on a floured surface and use your fingertips to tap the top around the outer edges and establish the base shape of the crust. (Tap your fingers like they are pouncing quickly on the dough.) This will form an edge or lip around the crust. Once you have your shape, gently pick up the dough and hold it like you would a steering wheel, leaving your thumbs under the lip of the crust so you don't press it thin. Start turning the pizza like you would a steering wheel, allowing the dough to hang down and brush the countertop as you rotate it. Carefully work it into an 8-inch round, occasionally using a closed fist to reshape it in the center. Stretching the dough this way, as opposed to rolling it out, keeps the dough from becoming tough and dense.

Traditional Italian Pepperoni Pizza *(continued)*

Once the crust is formed, place it on the prepared peel and set aside while you prep the pepperoni.

3. Put pepperoni slices between two paper towels and microwave 6 seconds on high. Pat out the grease. (This removes a little grease and dries out the pepperoni just a bit.)

4. Ladle as much sauce as desired over the crust and evenly spread it almost to the edges with the back of spoon or a rubber spatula. Top with desired amount of cheese, followed by the pepperoni slices.

5. Lift the pizza peel and hold it in the oven directly above your pizza stone or pan. (The front tip of the peel should be above the back edge of your pizza pan.) Gently jiggle the pizza peel back and forth as you pull it toward you and bring it out of the oven so the dough comes off the peel and onto the pan. Bake 3 to 5 minutes (but this will depend on how hot your oven gets; watching is far more important than time), until edges are golden brown.

Claire Tip:

One year I had a stuffed-crust pizza at a birthday party, and the next week, when my family made pizza, I asked my mom if we could make stuffed crust. But all we had was string cheese because the shredded cheese was going to be on the pizza. We sliced the string cheese in half and folded the crust around the pieces, and it worked perfectly.

Braised Short Ribs P. 162

MAIN
DISHES

ALL ABOUT CHICKEN

HOW LONG DO I BAKE CHICKEN?

For all my friends out there who are worried about serving undercooked chicken, here's a quick guide for how long to bake chicken:

- Whole chicken—roast at 375 degrees F. 1¼ to 2 hours, depending on the size of the bird (1½ hours for a 4 to 6 pound bird, or 15 to 18 minutes per pound)

- Chicken breasts—bake at 350 degrees F. 25 to 30 minutes

- Chicken thighs—bake at 425 degrees F. 30 to 35 minutes

- Chicken wings—bake at 400 degrees F. 45 minutes

HOW MUCH CHICKEN DO I NEED?

Chicken breasts are often quite large. One pound of chicken breasts should be enough for four people but may come packaged as only two breasts. If this is the case, cut the breasts into four pieces equal in size.

Two pounds of chicken is roughly equivalent to three large chicken breasts or four smaller breasts. You can cut the breasts into smaller pieces before or after cooking to serve more people.

NEED THINNER CHICKEN BREASTS?

To pound a breast thin, place it between two pieces of wax paper or plastic wrap and pound with a meat mallet until it's no thicker than ⅛ inch. Repeat with the other breasts. If you don't have a meat mallet, a heavy wooden rolling pin will work.

Or you can slice the chicken breasts through the middle, creating a butterfly as you open the two pieces of meat, then slice through to separate.

Perfect Chicken in a Pan

When I first started cooking, I always had to cut into my chicken to see if it was done. One of the most frustrating things to me is cooking a breast of chicken in a pan, believing that it is perfectly cooked, cutting in, and BAM! you've got a little pink in the center. I hated to cut into the chicken and ruin it.

But I did. Over and over again. I'd overcook it, undercook it, or end up slicing it in pieces and cooking those just in an attempt to get dinner on the table.

That hasn't happened to me in years. And here's the exact, perfectly foolproof way to get it right.

Prep: 5 min *Cook:* 14 min *Additional:* 3 min *Total:* 22 min *Yield:* 4 servings

1 pound boneless skinless chicken breasts

Salt and pepper, to taste (see note)

1 tablespoon olive oil or butter

1. Lay chicken breasts between 2 layers of wax paper or plastic wrap; use a meat mallet to pound breasts to a uniform ½-inch thickness. This will help the chicken cook more quickly and evenly.

2. Season each side of the chicken with salt and pepper.

3. Heat olive oil or butter in a large skillet over high heat. When oil starts to shimmer or butter begins foaming, lay chicken in the pan. Reduce heat to medium-low and let chicken cook 5 to 7 minutes. Flip chicken and cook another 5 to 7 minutes. Chicken is finished when no more pink remains and temperature registers 165 degrees F. on an instant-read thermometer.

4. Transfer chicken to a cutting board and let rest 3 minutes before serving or slicing for use in another recipe. This will trap the juices inside and make the chicken more tender. (If chicken—or any meat—is sliced immediately after cooking, the juices from the meat are released, resulting in a drier and less flavorful piece of meat.)

NOTE: You can experiment with many different seasonings in addition to the salt and pepper or in place of them—thyme, rosemary, specialty chicken seasonings, garlic powder, and so on.

3 Tips for Perfect Chicken

1. Keep a thermometer on hand—poultry is done at 165 degrees F.
2. Juices run clear when it's done.
3. Touch it: when firm and no longer a little jiggly in the center, it's done.

Chicken Noodle Soup

Homemade chicken noodle soup is the perfect recipe to teach a simple French cooking term and why it's essential. A *mirepoix* is a mix of aromatics made from finely diced vegetables. Onions, carrots, celery, and even garlic are cooked in butter or oil over low heat, which sweetens the ingredients versus caramelizing them.

I had already started making this soup one day when I realized I was out of onions. I hit the cupboard for garlic powder and noticed half an envelope of onion soup mix. On a whim, I threw it in—and, my goodness, it was amazing! The best chicken noodle soup recipe EVER came from a missing ingredient, but because it still added aromatics, it was a win!

Prep: 5 min *Cook:* 20 min *Total:* 25 min *Yield:* 6 to 8 servings

1 tablespoon olive oil

4 stalks celery, each cut in 3 vertical strips and then chopped

3 large carrots, sliced thin

½ (2-ounce) package dry onion soup mix

1½ teaspoons chopped fresh thyme leaves (or ¾ teaspoon dried)

2½ tablespoons minced fresh Italian parsley (or 1 tablespoon dried)

⅛ teaspoon ground nutmeg

2 tablespoons Better Than Bouillon Roasted Chicken Base (see note)

6 cups water (see note)

3 cups cooked and shredded chicken

12 ounces egg noodles

Salt, to taste

1. In a large pot, heat oil over medium heat until it begins to shimmer.
2. Add celery and carrots and sauté 2 minutes, stirring occasionally.
3. Add soup mix, thyme, parsley, and nutmeg. Cook and stir 20 to 30 seconds; quickly add Better Than Bouillon and water and then stir. Add the chicken and stir briefly.
4. Cover pot with lid and cook until carrots are tender, 20 to 30 minutes.
5. Increase temperature so mixture comes to a simmer. Drop in fresh pasta or dry noodles and season to taste with salt. Cook 1 to 2 minutes for fresh pasta; consult package directions for cook time of dry noodles. Once noodles are cooked, serve immediately.

NOTE: Substitute 6 cups chicken broth or stock for Better Than Bouillon and 6 cups water, if desired.

Pro Tip: Every fridge should always have a little cilantro and a little parsley. Start adding a little herbs, even to savory dishes right before serving and you'll be surprised by how much more delicious it turns out.

FEELING SALTY

Salting should happen before, during, and after cooking in almost every single recipe. Yes, even dessert. Salt adds flavor and balance and even accentuates the sweetness in a dish.

TYPES OF SALT

Table Salt is the most common salt you'll find. Head to your cupboard right now, pick it up, throw a little up in the air all "celebrity chef" style, and then summon your inner Michael Jordan and dunk it right in the ol' trash can.

Table salt is processed in a way that leads to a metallic aftertaste. You have to use more of it to get the flavor you want. And your food will never taste as good as you think it should.

Fine Sea Salt or Fine Grain Sea Salt is my favorite. I sometimes call it "real salt." It has fantastic flavor with absolutely no metallic aftertaste, so often you'll end up using less of it. This salt can be used in cooking and baking, but more often in baking.

Kosher Salt. In the "salt pig" that sits on the counter next to my stove 24/7 is a thicker grain of salt that adheres to food better than finer salt: kosher salt. Kosher salt can be used in both cooking and baking, although most chefs will use sea salt for baking and kosher for cooking.

SALTING MEAT

When steaks, roasts, or other cuts of meat end up tasting flavorless, it's usually because the meat wasn't properly prepared *prior* to cooking. Meat should always be salted prior to cooking.

The best-tasting meat comes from salting it, sticking it in the fridge uncovered (see time recommendations for different types of meat below), and then letting it sit on the counter to come closer to room temperature before cooking. Doing this creates a beautiful crust and gives you a deep, caramelized sear when panfrying. If you don't have time for that, be sure to at least thoroughly pat meat dry with paper towels and then salt it before cooking. The drier the meat, the better it will brown in the pan.

- Salt and refrigerate whole turkeys, prime rib, and whole pork butts 2 days before cooking.

- Salt and refrigerate whole chickens and thick steaks 24 hours before cooking.

- Salt and refrigerate other cuts of beef, pork, or poultry several hours the day of cooking.

- Salt seafood just before cooking.

SALTING VEGETABLES

Here are a few rules to follow when seasoning veggies:

- If you're steaming them in a pot, salt the water heavily (so salty you cringe when you taste it) right from the get-go.

- If you're roasting or grilling veggies, salt them just before putting them in the oven or on the grill.

- If you're sautéing them, season veggies after they have begun cooking, while in the pan.

- If you're serving them fresh, as with in-season tomatoes, salads, and the like, salt them right before bringing them to the table.

Slow Cooker Broccoli Cheese Soup

Is there anything better than a big ol' pot of soup on a dark, chilly, rainy day? Especially broccoli cheese soup—the perfect comfort food.

We went to Disneyland a while back, and my daughter Claire saw those huge bread bowls of soup and decided to jump in with both feet and try one. I cannot believe she ate the whole thing! We headed home and started making our own version together, which she loved! It's the creamiest, cheesiest slow cooker broccoli cheese soup you'll ever make. Best of all, you can change any of the cheeses to your own liking—like pepper jack, for more heat!

Prep: 15 min *Cook:* 3 hours *Additional:* 5 min
Total: 3 hours 20 min *Yield:* 6 servings

¼ cup butter

½ yellow onion, minced

2 cloves garlic, minced

1 carrot, peeled and grated

¼ cup all-purpose flour

4 ounces cream cheese, softened

3 cups chicken broth

1 cup heavy cream

2 cups whole milk

¼ teaspoon Worcestershire sauce

½ teaspoon ground nutmeg

½ teaspoon ground mustard

½ teaspoon dried thyme

3 teaspoons salt

½ teaspoon ground black pepper

4 cups chopped broccoli florets

2 cups shredded sharp cheddar cheese

⅓ cup grated Parmesan cheese

Bread bowls for serving (optional)

1. In a large saucepan over medium heat, melt butter until it foams. Add onion, garlic, and carrots and sauté, stirring occasionally, until onions are softened, about 5 minutes. Whisk in flour and cook 30 seconds. Add cream cheese and stir until melted.

2. Transfer mixture to the insert of a slow cooker. Add chicken broth, cream, milk, Worcestershire sauce, nutmeg, mustard, thyme, salt, pepper, and broccoli. Give it a quick stir, cover, and cook on low 5 to 6 hours or high 3 hours.

3. Ladle half of the soup into the jar of a blender and pulse 3 or 4 times. Return pureed mixture to slow cooker, stir in the cheeses, and serve.

Bottom of the Jar Chicken

I'm always looking for a quick and easy dinner recipe that anyone can make. I'd been taught long ago that a celebrity chef uses leftover jam from the bottom of the jar to make marinades for chicken and other poultry, and I knew that would be a perfect method to learn how to bake chicken.

I hope you and your family will love this simple but delish chicken recipe for many dinners to come.

Prep: 10 min   *Cook:* 30 min   *Total:* 40 min   *Yield:* 4 servings

4 medium-sized boneless skinless chicken breasts (about 1½ pounds)

⅓ cup apricot preserves (see note)

1⅓ cups Italian dressing

Dash garlic powder

1. Preheat the oven to 350 degrees F.
2. Arrange chicken breasts in an 8x8-inch baking dish. In a small bowl, whisk together preserves, salad dressing, and dash of garlic powder. Pour sauce over chicken and bake 25 to 30 minutes, until sauce is bubbly and chicken is cooked through. (If you're unsure, use a meat thermometer; it should be 165 degrees F. in the thickest part of the chicken.)
3. Serve chicken on its own or over cooked pasta. It also works well shredded in a salad.

NOTE: Feel free to try other flavors of preserves. Orange marmalade, apricot-pineapple preserves, and peach jam all work very well.

Grayson Tip:
Mom places the sauce ingredients in a jar with a lid and, because I'm so strong, she has me shake it up and pour it over the chicken. No mess, and I get to help!

Chicken Parmesan

My favorite recipe as a teen was chicken parmesan. Mom taught me all about browning chicken in a pan: butter gives flavor, but adding a little oil keeps everything from burning, as oil can cook at a higher temperature. She taught me the trick of using croutons for better flavor and texture with minimal effort and that there's nothing better than those bits of gooey cheese stuck to the sides of the pan.

Now my daughters are the ones sprinkling the cheese (often too heavy-handedly) as Grayson is clambering up the counters as fast as he can to snitch it, making the girls holler and this mama roll her eyes. The dynamics of family are forever, aren't they?

Prep: 15 min *Cook:* 20 min *Additional:* 1 hour 45 min (if preparing homemade marinara) *Total:* 35 min or 2 hours 20 min *Yield:* 4 servings

1 bag focaccia or garden herb croutons, crushed (see note)

2 boneless skinless chicken breasts, pounded flat and cut in half to make 4 pieces

1 tablespoon butter

1 tablespoon olive oil

1 jar bottled marinara sauce

2 cups shredded mozzarella cheese

1 pound angel hair pasta

1. Preheat oven to 350 degrees F. Spray a 9x13-inch pan or 3-quart baking dish with non-stick cooking spray. Place crushed croutons in a shallow bowl.

2. Dredge both sides of each chicken breast in the crushed croutons and set pieces on a clean platter while heating skillet.

3. Melt butter in a large skillet over medium heat. When butter begins to foam, add olive oil and heat until pan sizzles when a drop of water is dropped in.

4. Lay breasts in hot skillet and cook on each side 2 to 3 minutes, until golden. Do not crowd the pan. If needed, cook breasts in batches. Transfer breasts to prepared baking dish.

5. Pour marinara sauce evenly over chicken breasts and top with shredded cheese. Bake 20 minutes, until sauce is bubbly and cheese is beginning to brown.

6. Meanwhile, prepare pasta according to package directions. Remove chicken from oven. Plate with a little pasta topped with marinara. Place your cheesy chicken on top and enjoy.

NOTE: To crush croutons, place croutons in a large zip-top bag, seal bag, and use a rolling pin or meat mallet to pound the croutons. You can use seasoned panko bread crumbs in place of the croutons if needed.

COOKING AS A FAMILY

As you're making mealtime a priority in your home, remember, cooking dinner does not have to be overwhelming. Take it one step at a time, clean as you go, and make sure everyone pitches in.

At the beginning of each week, we pull out a paper and make a list of some of the things we want to cook that week. (Except for the weeks when we don't do this—no family is perfect.) Each family member picks something he or she will make (or helps make), anything from dinner to dessert.

Next, we quickly jot down any groceries we need to buy. Later, I do the shopping, or I take the kids with me to the store and have them help me find the ingredients we're missing so they can learn to pick out food with confidence instead of being overwhelmed by the grocery store.

In the beginning, things might go slowly. But here are your choices: cook for your whole life until you die, or teach your kids to cook so that by the time they are twelve they are making you meals.

Little Kids: Cook with help.

Older Kids: Cook more on their own with a parent as a sous chef to help.

Teens: Cook meals alone with a parent to supervise if needed.

Making the effort in the beginning—including teaching them to respect the kitchen by also cleaning up—*always* pays off later.

Be careful not to say yes to everything the kids ask to make. Saying yes to everything is overwhelming and often leads to everyone feeling stressed and the kitchen getting extra messy. Maybe, on a busy week, I will tell Claire, "It's not a good week to make that dish, so I'll save it for another week while you think up something else." When I need to say no, I talk in upbeat ways, subtly redirect the conversation, and give praise and encouragement—a lot, and often.

After the planning and shopping are done, a weekly meal plan might look like this:

MONDAY: GRAYSON
Chicken Tortilla Soup *(page 134)*

TUESDAY: MOM
Chocolate Smoothie Bowl
(page 7) and popcorn

WEDNESDAY: PEYTON
Garlic Butter Steaks *(page 160)*

THURSDAY: MOM
Fall-Off-the-Bone Oven-Baked Ribs
(page 139)

FRIDAY: MOM
Pizza Night *(page 115)*

SATURDAY: DAD / CLAIRE
Yogurt Cups for breakfast *(page 9)*
Smothered Chicken Burritos
for dinner *(page 149)*

SUNDAY: MOM
Pasta Bolognese *(page 105)*

And finally: Did everyone eat the food? Then everyone helps clean up the food. It hasn't ever worked for us to assign a kid a night for dishes.

Cleaning solo is overwhelming even for many adults, and it takes longer. After a meal is over, each person clears their own dishes and then help clean up everything else, including wiping down counters and sweeping up if needed, which it always is. Everything is better when you do it together, especially when Grandpa and Grandma come to visit so we can get back to playing together.

Our family has timed it for you. Our quickest cleanup took 3 minutes and 36 seconds, and the longest took 14 minutes and 12 seconds.

Chicken Tortilla Soup

For years I've been making every chicken tortilla soup recipe out there and not really getting excited about any. Until now. It all starts with a flavorful base of all kinds of veggies that is blended smooth and totally flavorful. Then we add all your favorite chunky tortilla soup essentials and top it with crunchy tortilla strips, slices of avocado, and more cheese!

Prep: 25 min   *Cook:* 30 min   *Total:* 55 min   *Yield:* 8 to 10 servings

1 tablespoon olive oil

½ onion, chopped

1 large carrot, peeled and chopped

1 stalk celery, chopped

1 red bell pepper, chopped

1½ teaspoons garlic powder

3 teaspoons taco seasoning

2 Roma tomatoes, quartered

1 (15-ounce) can fire-roasted diced tomatoes, drained

1 (4-ounce) can fire-roasted diced green chiles, drained

½ avocado, plus more (sliced) for serving

⅓ cup shredded Monterey Jack or Mexican cheese, plus more for serving

1 (15-ounce) can black beans, drained and divided

10 tortilla chips, plus more for serving

3 cups cooked and shredded chicken

1½ to 2 cups frozen corn

2 cups low-sodium chicken broth

2 cups water

1½ teaspoons kosher salt

¼ cup chopped fresh cilantro

Claire Tip:
Sometimes when we make this, we double the veggies and store the extras in the freezer so it goes faster the next time.

1. In a large Dutch oven or soup pot, heat oil over medium heat until it begins to shimmer. Add onions, carrots, celery, and bell pepper. Reduce heat to low and cook until veggies are tender, about 10 minutes.

2. Stir in garlic powder, taco seasoning, Roma tomatoes, canned tomatoes, and green chiles. Cook, stirring occasionally, 8 to 10 minutes to allow flavors to meld.

3. Transfer veggie mixture to the jar of blender. Add avocado and cheese. Puree until completely smooth, about 1 minute. Add ½ of the black beans and 10 tortilla chips. Pulse just a few times so there are some chunks left.

4. Pour mixture back into the pot. Add cooked chicken, remaining black beans, corn, broth, water, and salt. Cook and simmer over medium heat 30 minutes, stirring occasionally and reducing heat as needed if soup starts to boil.

5. Just before serving, stir in the cilantro. Serve topped with avocado slices, chips, and cheese.

Mexican Cheesy Rice Casserole

This is one of our most popular recipes, and it's great for picky eaters, too.

I grew up on casseroles. My grandma made my mom casseroles, my mom made them for me, and now we both laugh about how something this simple can make us feel so at home. (Doesn't everyone need a simple recipe that reminds them of home?) I always get nostalgic when I make or eat a casserole. I hope whether it's a cold, wintry day or a blazing scorcher in July, you'll settle down at the dinner table with a heaping plate of Mexican Cheesy Rice Casserole and feel like you're at home.

Prep: **15 min**   *Cook:* **1 hour 33 min**   *Total:* **1 hour 48 min**   *Yield:* **6 servings**

1 pound ground beef

1 (1-ounce) packet taco seasoning mix

2¾ cups water, divided

1 (11-ounce) can Campbell's Condensed Fiesta Nacho Cheese Soup

1 cup long-grain white rice

1 (15-ounce) can black beans, drained

9 slices cheddar or Colby Jack cheese

Salsa, for serving (page 67)

Avocados, sliced, for serving

1. Preheat oven to 350 degrees F. Spray an 8×8-inch baking dish with nonstick cooking spray.
2. In a large skillet over medium heat, cook ground beef, using a wooden spoon to break up meat, until browned and no more pink remains, 10 to 12 minutes. Drain off fat and return pan to stovetop.
3. Stir in taco seasoning and ¾ cup water. Bring to a boil, then reduce heat and simmer 5 minutes, stirring occasionally.
4. Add remaining water, condensed soup, rice, and beans and stir to combine well.
5. Transfer mixture to prepared baking dish and bake 90 minutes. Top casserole with cheese slices and bake until cheese melts, about 3 more minutes.
6. Serve topped with a dollop of salsa and a few avocado slices.

NOTE: This recipe can easily be doubled and baked in a 9x13-inch pan. The baking time remains the same.

Fall-Off-the-Bone Oven-Baked Ribs

The first time I visited the South, I couldn't believe that a dry rub was all that it took to make perfect, fall-off-the-bone ribs. Good flavor and proper cooking make for the best ribs! I coat my ribs in a bold dry rub and then cook them low and slow to mouth-watering perfection.

Prep: 15 min   *Cook:* 3 to 4 hours   *Total:* 4 hours 15 min   *Yield:* 6 servings

Dry Rub

¼ cup smoked paprika

½ cup dark brown sugar

1 tablespoon black pepper

1 tablespoon garlic powder

2 teaspoon cumin

1 tablespoon kosher salt

1 teaspoon cayenne

Ribs

2 racks pork spare ribs or baby back

½ cup Dijon mustard

½ cup apple cider, divided

½ cup dark brown sugar

⅓ cup honey

1. In a medium bowl, mix all ingredients for the dry rub together and set aside.

2. Check the bone-side of ribs, and remove silver skin if necessary. (Work the tip of a butter knife underneath the membrane, then pierce it over a middle bone. Grip silver skin firmly with a paper towel and tear off the membrane.)

3. In a small bowl, combine mustard and ¼ cup apple cider. Spread mixture thinly on both sides of ribs. Season with dry rub.

4. Heat oven to 275 degrees F. Wrap ribs tightly in foil—use a top and a bottom piece for easy opening later—and place ribs on a baking sheet. Cook ribs, meat-side up, for 2½ hours.

5. Remove from oven and carefully open foil to expose the ribs.

6. Sprinkle brown sugar evenly over ribs. Mix honey and remaining apple cider together and divide evenly over both racks of ribs.

7. Cook ribs an additional 1 to 1 ½ hours, depending on how tender you like your meat.

8. Remove foil from ribs, and increase oven temperature to 500 degrees F. Cook ribs until outside is crispy, anywhere from 1 to 4 minutes, then remove from oven.

9. Brush with your favorite barbeque sauce, if desired.

NOTE: The Best Potato Salad recipe on page 90 is the perfect side for these ribs. See ohsweetbasil.com for our Traeger Smoked Ribs variation.

Teriyaki Chicken Quesadilla

I know this is a little weird to admit, but I might as well let you in on my life. So here goes: at least three or four times a week, when I would get home from high school, I'd make myself a teriyaki chicken quesadilla or burrito. I know, dinner was only a few hours away, but while most kids were having a snack, I was having a full-on meal.

Teriyaki chicken stuffed in a cheesy quesadilla—it doesn't get much better than that! I love the sweet and tangy flavor of teriyaki, but then wrap it in gooey, melty cheese and a buttery tortilla, and you have yourself an out-of-this-world meal!

Prep: 30 min   *Cook:* 45 min   *Total:* 1 hour 15 min   *Yield:* 2 to 4 servings

¾ cup low-sodium soy sauce

½ cup water

⅓ cup brown sugar

1 tablespoon honey

¾ teaspoon ground ginger

1 teaspoon sesame oil

1 clove garlic, finely minced

2 tablespoons cornstarch

2 tablespoons cold water

1 large boneless skinless chicken breast (about 6 to 8 ounces)

4 uncooked flour tortillas (page 45)

2 cups shredded cheddar cheese

Claire and Grayson Tip:
We love making quesadillas. You already know how to make a sauce, how to make chicken, and how to make tortillas. We think this is the perfect time to experiment with combining flavors. Try making a pizza quesadilla or a BBQ pulled pork version. Just be sure that if you put meat in the middle, you sprinkle a little extra cheese on, as the meat keeps the tortilla open more.

1. Preheat oven to 350 degrees F. Spray a 2-quart baking dish or an 8x8-inch pan with nonstick cooking spray; set aside.

2. In a medium saucepan over medium-high heat, stir together soy sauce, ½ cup water, brown sugar, honey, ground ginger, sesame oil, and garlic. Bring to a boil and cook 1 minute, stirring occasionally.

3. In a small bowl, whisk together cornstarch and 2 tablespoons cold water. Add 1 teaspoon of the hot soy mixture to the cornstarch mixture, mix well, and then slowly pour cornstarch mixture into the boiling soy mixture. Whisk until sauce begins to thicken, 8 to 10 minutes; remove from heat and set aside.

4. Place chicken breasts in prepared dish and pour sauce over top. Bake until chicken is cooked through and registers 165 degrees F. on an instant-read thermometer, about 30 minutes. (In a hurry? Slice the chicken and heat a skillet over medium-high heat, cooking the chicken

Hot Kitchen Hints!

- Make sure you always use a dry towel or pot holder when grabbing something hot. A wet one will let the heat right through the fibers and cause you to burn your hands.
- When adding food to hot water, always gently place it in so water won't splash up and burn you.
- When adding food to hot oil, keep your hands close to the oil and gently place the food in before quickly pulling your hands back. If you drop the food in hard and fast, the oil can start a fire or burn your hands.
- Never wash hot pans; it can ruin them.
- Whenever you're cooking, set timers so you don't burn food. It's also helpful to set a timer when a recipe calls for flipping or turning something after a set amount of time.
- When you're finished cooking, always check twice that you've turned off all ovens and burners.

while turning the pieces often, 5 to 7 minutes.)

5. Transfer chicken to a plate, reserving the sauce in the pan, and shred with 2 forks; set aside.

6. In a nonstick skillet over medium heat, cook both sides of each tortilla according to package directions; remove from pan.

7. To assemble each quesadilla, sprinkle ¼ cup cheese over a tortilla, followed by half of the shredded chicken. Drizzle a spoonful or 2 of the reserved sauce over the chicken and sprinkle with another ¼ cup cheese. Top with another tortilla and return to skillet over medium heat.

8. Cook 3 to 4 minutes, flipping once, until cheese is melted. Repeat with remaining ingredients.

9. Use a pizza cutter or a very sharp knife to cut each quesadilla into 4 wedges. Serve immediately.

Cafe Rio Chicken Salad

This slow cooker Cafe Rio Chicken copycat recipe is seriously so good, and if you don't want to do a salad, then turn it into a chicken burrito! I love that you can throw everything together in less than 5 minutes, let it cook all day, and then feel like a hero as you serve it to your family.

Need a great dinner idea to take to someone with a new baby, or a family-friendly meal? Try this chicken served with cilantro lime rice. Best of all, it's the easiest way to learn how to use a blender, slow cooker, and rice cooker all at once.

Prep: 15 min   *Cook:* 5 hours   *Total:* 5 hours 15 min   *Yield:* 6 to 8 servings

5 pounds boneless skinless chicken breasts

1 (16-ounce) bottle Kraft Zesty Italian Dressing

1 tablespoon ground cumin

1 tablespoon chili powder

3 cloves garlic, minced

Tortillas (page 45)

For Assembly

Cilantro Lime Rice (page 145)

1 (15-ounce) can black beans, drained and cooked

2 heads romaine lettuce, chopped

Guacamole

Shredded cheese

Salsa

Creamy Tomatillo Cilantro Ranch Dressing (page 145)

1. Spray insert of a slow-cooker with nonstick cooking spray and layer chicken breasts in insert. In a liquid measuring cup or medium bowl, whisk together Italian dressing, cumin, chili powder, and garlic. Pour mixture over chicken and cook on low 4 hours. Transfer chicken to a large bowl, leaving the sauce in the slow cooker, and shred. Return shredded chicken to slow cooker and cook an additional 1 hour.

2. To assemble salads, divide lettuce between plates or bowls and top with a generous scoop of shredded chicken, some Cilantro Lime Rice, and additional toppings. Serve with Creamy Tomatillo Cilantro Ranch Dressing on the side.

Claire Tip:
I like making my own and usually turn it into a burrito or quesadilla instead of a salad.

Cafe Rio Chicken Salad *(continued)*

Cilantro Lime Rice

Prep: 5 min *Cook:* 30 min *Total:* 35 min *Yield:* 6 to 8 servings

2 cups long-grain white rice

4 cups water

2 tablespoons unsalted butter

2 teaspoons granulated chicken
   bouillon

1 clove garlic, minced

1 handful cilantro, chopped

½ lime, juiced

1 (4-ounce) can diced green chiles

Add all ingredients to a large saucepan and stir to combine. Bring mixture to a boil over high heat, cover with lid, and reduce heat to low. Let cook 20 to 30 minutes. Remove lid, fluff rice with a fork, and serve immediately.

Creamy Tomatillo Cilantro Ranch Dressing

Time: 15 min *Yield:* 2½ to 3 cups

1 jalapeño pepper (for a milder
   dressing, remove seeds)

1 clove garlic

1 tomatillo, husked and halved

1 handful cilantro

Juice from 1 lime

1 cup milk

1 (1-ounce) packet ranch dressing and
   seasoning mix

1 cup mayonnaise

1. Add jalapeño, garlic, tomatillo, cilantro, lime juice, milk, and ranch dressing mix to the jar of a blender and process until smooth.

2. Pour mixture into a medium bowl and whisk in mayo until well combined. Cover with plastic wrap and refrigerate until ready to use. Before using, whisk to recombine. Can be refrigerated in an airtight container up to 2 weeks.

Pro Tip: I always think about dinner at least a day ahead. The night before or morning of if you find yourself with ten minutes, go ahead and prep ahead, shred cheese, chop tomatoes, and whisk together the sauce. Just store everything in the fridge and your dinnertime will be a breeze.

Likewise, I love to make doubles of ingredients and store the other half for a busy day. For example, rotisserie chicken can be shredded and frozen for up to 3 months, and rice can be cooked, placed in zip-top bags, and laid flat in the freezer for up to 5 months.

Garlic-Parmesan Chicken and Rice

I was talking on the phone with my mom once while making this chicken, and when I took my first bite, I said, "Mom! This is the best chicken and rice EVER! It's so much better than any other brown rice."

Mom said, "Oh, I wish I could come to dinner at your house."

When did I become the adult cooking the dinners? Do we always have to grow up? One day you might have kids of your own, if you don't already, and you'll get it. You'll get how you feel about them and how you feel about your mom. Oh, to be sitting on her counter with feet dangling one more time!

Prep: 10 min *Cook:* 50 min *Total:* 1 hour *Yield:* 4 to 6 servings

½ cup freshly grated Parmesan cheese, plus more for garnishing

4 large cloves garlic, minced and divided

1 teaspoon smoked paprika

1 teaspoon Italian seasoning

2 pounds boneless skinless chicken breasts

Salt and pepper, to taste

4 tablespoons unsalted butter, divided

2 cups brown rice

4 cups chicken broth

Zest of 1 lemon

Juice of 1 lemon

¼ teaspoon salt

¼ teaspoon ground black pepper

2 tablespoons chopped fresh parsley

1. In a shallow dish or pie pan, combine Parmesan cheese, half of the minced garlic, paprika, and Italian seasoning. Season each chicken breast to taste with salt and pepper then dredge in Parmesan mixture. Shake off excess and let chicken rest on a plate.

2. Melt 2 tablespoons butter in skillet over medium-high heat. Add remaining garlic and sauté until fragrant, about 30 seconds. Quickly add the rice and stir continuously 1 minute, just until the edges of the rice start to turn translucent. Stir in broth, lemon zest and juice, ¼ teaspoon salt, and ¼ teaspoon pepper and bring to a boil.

3. Reduce heat to medium-low, cover, and cook until rice is tender and no liquid remains, about 40 minutes.

4. Meanwhile, in a large skillet, melt remaining 2 tablespoons of the butter over medium-high heat. When butter starts to foam, tilt pan so it evenly coats the bottom. Add chicken to pan and cook until golden brown and cooked through, 4 to 6 minutes per side.

5. Fluff rice with a fork. Nestle chicken atop rice, cover with the lid, and warm everything together.

6. Serve topped with fresh chopped parsley and extra Parmesan cheese.

Smothered Chicken Burritos

There was this restaurant near my college campus called New York Burrito. It was a build-your-own-burrito spot, and I loved to go there with my roommate and make up our own concoctions, then head back home to devour them while we watched TV. Since the burritos were big enough for two meals, I'd hurry home after class the next day to stuff my face with my leftover burrito. I still think there's something particularly fulfilling about eating a burrito, especially a smothered version.

Prep: 15 min   *Marinate:* 20 min   *Cook:* 20 min   *Total:* 55 min   *Yield:* 8 burritos

¼ cup lime juice

⅓ cup honey

6 cloves garlic, minced

1 tablespoon chili powder

2 to 3 cups cooked and shredded rotisserie chicken

2 cups prepared Cilantro Lime Rice (page 145)

1 (16-ounce) jar Herdez Salsa Verde

1 cup heavy cream, or to taste

8 burrito-sized flour tortillas

1 (15.5-ounce) can pinto beans, drained and warmed

1 to 2 cups shredded Colby Jack cheese

1 to 2 cups shredded mozzarella cheese

Pico de gallo, for garnishing

Chopped fresh cilantro, for garnishing

Sour cream, for garnishing

1. Preheat oven to 350 degrees F.

2. In a large bowl, whisk together lime juice, honey, garlic, and chili powder. Add shredded chicken and toss to coat. Cover bowl with plastic wrap and refrigerate 15 to 30 minutes. (If you didn't prepare the Cilantro Lime Rice in advance, do so while chicken marinates.)

3. In a medium bowl, whisk together jarred salsa verde and heavy cream; set aside. (The more cream you add, the less spicy it will be.)

4. Warm tortillas by placing the stack in a towel in the microwave for 20 seconds, or heat individually in a pan over medium-high heat.

5. To assemble burritos, spread ¼ cup rice down the middle of a tortilla, followed by a spoonful of warmed beans, ¼ to ⅓ cup chicken, and 2 to 4 tablespoons shredded Colby Jack cheese. Fold up both ends and roll tightly to close.

6. Place the burritos on a rimmed baking sheet and spoon a generous helping of sauce over each. Top with shredded mozzarella cheese, adjusting the amount to your taste. Bake 20 to 30 minutes, until cheese is melted and burritos are warmed through. Serve garnished with pico de gallo, chopped cilantro, and sour cream.

Peyton Tip:
You can freeze little burritos for an after-school snack. Just make up small ones at dinner, wrap in tinfoil twice, and put in a zip-top bag in the freezer for a few weeks. To reheat, just unwrap it on a plate and microwave.

ABOUT MEAT

If I could shout this one from the rooftops, I would: never slice or cut into meat straight out of the oven or off the stovetop. Let it rest! If you don't, you'll lose all the delicious juices in the meat that make it tender and flavorful. Letting chicken, beef, and pork rest allows the juices to be reabsorbed into the meat and makes the finished product moist and tender. Smaller cuts, such as chicken breasts, need only 5 minutes to rest. Bigger cuts need 20 to 30 minutes, and the biggest cuts—like a whole pork butt—may need to rest as long as an hour.

HOW TO BUY A ROAST

- Look for a dark red color in the meat and a thick covering of fat and marbling throughout the meat, which adds flavor and prevents the meat from drying out during cooking. Darker color equals richer flavor. There shouldn't be any brown.

- If you are buying a cut that is meant to be tender with plenty of marbling, such as a rib eye, the marbling should be consistent through the meat.

- The best roast is a tenderloin, but because of its higher price tag, I generally stick with buying a top round roast or chuck roast.

- Plan on needing ½ pound of boneless meat per adult and ¼ pound per child.

MEATS IN THE SLOW COOKER

Chicken breasts and smaller meats only need about 4 hours on low or 3 hours on high.

Bigger meats, like a roast or ribs, generally need about 8 hours on low. I would never cook a roast on high. The bigger the meat, the more time you need to make it tender. Slow and low allows the fats to render out and the meat fibers to loosen. No sliced beef here; it will fall apart on its own.

GRILLING

Start by heating a gas grill to high heat. This is important for grill marks and caramelization. After a while, place your hand, palm flattened, about 5 inches above the grill and count how long it takes before you can no longer hold it there comfortably. For high heat, you won't be able to hold it there more than 2 seconds. Medium heat is 4 to 6 seconds. Add the meat and quickly adjust grill to the desired temperature.

The most important thing about grilling meats is actually not about the grill at all. It's about the time right *after* you pull the meat off of the grill. With the exception of seafood, meats should be rested after cooking. So, pull out a cutting board or platter, place the meat on it, and allow it to rest before ever slicing it.

BRAISING

To braise meat means to cook it slowly in the oven with a little liquid added to the roaster or baking pan.

Here's why it works: the long, slow, moist heat that happens in a pot with a lid is the best way to soften beans and meat. Adding tomato products, which are very acidic, helps break down the tough fibers of the beans or connective tissues in meat.

Give braising a shot by making Braised Short Ribs on page 162.

MARINATING MYTHS

MYTH: *Marinating is the key to flavorful meat all the way through.*

TRUTH: Marinating happens only to the very outer edges of the meat. Marinades on meat, especially tough cuts like a flank steak for carne asada, add flavor and tenderize the meat.

MYTH: *Marinating alone is sufficient for flavor.*

TRUTH: Always reserve a little marinade to add at the end of cooking or just before serving for ultimate flavor.

MYTH: *Marinades should include herbs in order to be flavorful.*

TRUTH: The best marinades are made by using salt, sugar, oil, and an acid, such as lemon or vinegar. These components help to tenderize the meat and add flavor. Herbs cannot penetrate the meat deeply enough to flavor it on their own; add them, for sure, but know the flavor isn't coming solely from the herbs.

MYTH: *The longer you marinate meat the better.*

TRUTH: Soak your chicken, pork chops, or seafood at least 30 minutes, but never longer than 8 hours. Steak can handle resting in a marinade up to overnight, but never push anything over 24 hours.

Slow Cooker Pot Roast

Raising a family of five kids, especially with at least one picky eater (me), couldn't have been easy. In fact, it must have been exhausting and expensive. It's probably why so many Sundays at my house included a slow cooker pot roast with potatoes and carrots, which fed a lot of us with minimal work.

No matter what your family size is, mealtime can be a bit of a chore, but it doesn't have to be. A recipe that takes all day is actually a blessing, as you can set it and forget it. And best of all, it's a recipe that each person can take a piece of: you peel and chop carrots, you do the potatoes, and I'll do the meat.

Prep: 5 min   *Cook:* 8 hours   *Total:* 8 hours 5 min   *Yield:* 6 to 8 servings

1 (3-pound) beef chuck roast

1 (1-ounce) packet ranch dressing and seasoning mix

1 (1-ounce) packet au jus gravy mix

½ cup (1 stick) unsalted butter

1. Spray insert of slow cooker with nonstick cooking spray.

2. Place roast in insert and sprinkle top with ranch seasoning mix. Sprinkle au jus mix over that and then place the whole stick of butter on top.

3. Cook on low 8 hours. Remove lid 30 minutes before cooking time ends, and shred meat with 2 forks, mixing it into the liquid as you do. Return lid and cook remaining 30 minutes.

NOTE: To make a gravy, pour drippings from insert into a small saucepan and bring to a boil over medium-high heat. If drippings are scarce, add 1 cup water. In a small bowl, mix together 1 table-spoon cornstarch with 1 tablespoon water and add to drippings. Whisk again and cook until mixture bubbles. Reduce heat and sim-mer until thickened.

Pro Tip: Searing does not seal in the juices. Searing only adds caramelization and flavor. A slow cooker roast is more delicious if you sear it, but it's not necessary to do so.

Steak Fajitas

I love it when Taco Tuesday falls on Cinco de Mayo. It's like the world could implode with that much serendipity. It doesn't matter who you are, Mexican food speaks to the soul. It's good, it's comforting, and it's easy. Marinate some meat, flip to our homemade tortillas recipe, and bust out a meal your family will be drooling over!

Prep: 2 hours *Cook:* 25 min *Total:* 2 hours 25 min *Yield:* 4 to 6 fajitas or 6 to 8 tacos

2 pounds flank steak (see sidebar for grilling directions)

3 tablespoons plus 2 teaspoons olive or canola oil, divided

¼ cup orange juice

¼ cup lime juice

¼ cup pineapple juice

2 tablespoons Worcestershire sauce

4 cloves garlic, minced

2½ teaspoons ground cumin

2 teaspoons chili powder

1 teaspoon smoked paprika

¼ teaspoon ground coriander

2 teaspoons kosher salt

½ teaspoon ground black pepper

⅓ cup chopped fresh cilantro

1 tablespoon butter

1 red bell pepper, sliced

1 yellow bell pepper, sliced

1 orange bell pepper, sliced

1 green bell pepper, sliced

1 onion, sliced

1 teaspoon taco seasoning

1. Place steak in a gallon-sized zip-top bag. Depending on your preferred cooking method, either leave the steak whole for the grill or slice it for the pan.

2. In a medium bowl, whisk together 3 tablespoons oil, fruit juices, Worcestershire sauce, garlic, cumin, chili powder, paprika, coriander, salt, pepper, and cilantro. Reserve and refrigerate ¼ cup of the marinade. Pour remaining marinade over the steak in the zip-top bag. Seal bag, shake to coat steak, and marinate in refrigerator 2 to 24 hours.

3. When ready to prepare fajitas, heat 1 teaspoon oil in a cast-iron skillet (a nonstick skillet will also work). Add butter, and heat until butter begins to foam and pan is very hot. Add pepper slices, onion slices, and taco seasoning. Stir briefly, then reduce heat to medium-low and cook, stirring occasionally, until onions are golden brown and peppers are tender, about 20 minutes. Transfer cooked onions and peppers to a large bowl.

4. (If you prefer to grill your steak, refer to grilling directions in the sidebar.) Add another 1 to 2 teaspoons oil to the pan and increase heat to medium-high. Remove steak slices from zip-top bag and shake off excess marinade. (Discard used marinade.) When oil begins to shimmer, add steak to hot pan and cook 2 minutes without moving. Flip

Grilling Your Steak

1. Do not slice the meat before marinating.

2. Reserve ¼ cup of the marinade in the refrigerator, then put the whole flank steak in a zip-top bag and pour remaining marinade over top. Seal bag and refrigerate 2 to 24 hours.

3. Once peppers and onions are cooking on the stovetop, heat grill to high. (If using a charcoal grill, arrange coals and heat the grill so that one side gets high, direct heat, and the other gets low heat.) Remove whole flank steak from marinade, letting excess marinade drip back into the bag.

4. Discard used marinade and cut the steak in half widthwise. Place the thicker half of the steak on hot grill. Grill 2 minutes, then add the thinner half of the steak to the grill. Grill both for another 2 to 4 minutes on each side, just until sear marks form.

5. Reduce heat to medium or, if using a charcoal grill, move steak to the other side of the grill. Baste steak with reserved marinade and cook 4 to 6 minutes per side, depending on how well-done you like your steak. Cook to 125 degrees F. for rare meat, 135 degrees F. for medium rare, or 145 degrees F. for medium.

6. Move steak to cutting board and tent with aluminum foil. Let rest 5 minutes, then slice and add to pan with onions and peppers.

7. Cook and stir 1 minute to meld flavors.

slices and cook another 2 to 3 minutes, depending on how well-done you like your steak.

5. Reduce heat to low and return peppers and onions to pan. Drizzle mixture with reserved ¼ cup marinade, then cook and stir just until everything is warmed through, about 1 minute. Serve immediately over warm flour tortillas for fajitas or as the filling for tacos, using your favorite soft or hard-shell taco shells.

PICKY EATERS?

I was the worst child to please in the kitchen. I'm sure my mouth was perpetually pinched shut and my mind was saying, *I'm hungry, except for anything you made.*

Are you picky? Is someone you know picky? (I'm looking at you, Grayson.) If it's not pizza, crepes, or Chick-fil-A, my boy probably isn't all that interested. No, that's not true: he's a snacker as well—bring on the pretzels!

It seems like we are constantly working on squashing picky eating at our house. When I tell my mom and dad about our struggles, they always give me a mischievous smirk—as if somehow they prayed the picky eaters upon me just because I was such a nightmare growing up.

And friends, it didn't end until I got married. So there is hope.

Here are a few tips to help your kids (or maybe you) overcome picky eating:

1. Plan meals and grocery shop together. I've found that planning meals together and grocery shopping as a team helps a picky eater feel more invested in the food they are eating. In addition, the picky eater has at least one safe day that they chose what to eat, which allows them to feel more willing to power through the unknown days.

2. Use small plates and tiny portions. Kids are little; don't overwhelm them!

3. "Kiss it or lick it." My friend Lisa taught me this one for my picky eater. Getting comfortable feeling the food with their tongue can often help them finally take a bite.

4. Place something familiar on the plate but with the rule that they can't eat it until they have tried one bite of each new thing on the plate. Our little guy doesn't like anything new or different, but having something familiar alongside the new food helps his plate still feel approachable.

5. Make a chart and award a sticker each time they eat dinner without complaining to earn a reward. Start with a weekly reward and move up until it's a monthly reward.

6. Stop offering options. If they won't eat dinner, don't break out the cereal. You're only solidifying that they don't have to eat your food.

7. Use constant praise. Try clapping and praising when necessary to help your picky eater feel proud that they accomplished something.

KNIFE SKILLS 101

Never place your forefinger on top of the knife blade and grip the knife handle with your other fingers. This is not stable and will lead to accidents.

Instead, using your thumb and forefinger, pinch the knife blade, not just the handle, but the blade, or grip the bolster—that's the chunky part between the handle and blade.

For the hand holding the food, always tuck in your fingernails, curving your hand like you're holding a baseball. (Or think about a tarantula, the creepiest spider in my opinion. Those legs are tall and curled under; make your hand look like that.) Press the side of the knife's blade against your knuckles as you work. This will protect those dainty digits from being injured.

Make a circular motion, up and down, as you cut, never allowing the tip of the knife to leave the board. Just gently lift and lower the blade up and down to chop through the food. It's all about maintaining control.

Most recipes call for cutting meats, vegetables, fruit, or herbs in one of four specific sizes: chopped, small diced, minced, or sliced.

HOW TO DICE OR CHOP AN ONION

1. Start by holding the knife as described above.
2. Slice the onion horizontally from stem to root, without cutting through the root, by placing your hand wide open on top of the onion and pressing down with the palm of your hand to hold it in place.
3. Repeat, moving upward to slice layers into the onion. Slice vertically, stopping before the root.
4. Slice at a 90-degree angle through the onion in a chop or dice size.

HOW TO SLICE AN ONION

1. Trim off the top end of the onion (opposite of the root).
2. Stand the onion up on the cut end and cut in half, going straight through the root. The root helps to hold the onion together as you are chopping.
3. Peel off the outside layer of the onion.
4. Remove root end at a 45-degree angle.
5. Slice, following the faint lines and curvature on the onion. Do not cut straight down.

HOW TO CHOP HERBS

Gather the herbs into a ball in the fingers of one hand, and slice through them from one end of the ball to the next.

Place the hand that was holding the herbs on top of the knife and use a rocking motion to chop through all of the herbs.

SLICED, DICED, AND CHOPPED

The purple onion on the left is diced, because the pieces are slightly smaller than the chopped pieces in the middle. The food on the right has been sliced into thin rounds.

Garlic Butter Steak

Have you ever had a steak so perfectly cooked and seasoned that it literally (and I know this doesn't seem possible, but I mean literally) melts in your mouth? Oh, man, it's like nothing can ever compare to a steak like that again! This Garlic Butter Steak is just that kind of steak, but you can make it without ever leaving your house.

Prep: 30 min   *Cook:* 10 min   *Total:* 40 min   *Yield:* 3 servings

Garlic Butter

½ cup (1 stick) unsalted butter, at room temperature

3 cloves garlic, minced

½ teaspoon kosher salt

¼ teaspoon ground black pepper

1. With an electric mixer, combine all ingredients in a medium bowl until they are well incorporated and butter is smooth.

2. Lay a piece of parchment paper on the counter and transfer butter mixture to paper; shape into a log like a stick of butter. Roll parchment around shaped butter, twisting the paper at both ends to close. Refrigerate until ready to use, up to 1 week.

Steak

Garlic Butter

3 (12-ounce) rib eye steaks, cut 1¼ inches thick

4 tablespoons olive oil

Kosher salt and fresh ground black pepper, to taste

Pro Tip: Steaks can be tricky to buy. Rib eye steaks are one of the most flavorful cuts, but a a filet or New York strip also works well cooked this way.

1. Set Garlic Butter out on countertop to soften slightly. Preheat oven to broil. Place a cast-iron skillet or other oven-safe skillet on the center rack of the oven to heat while you prepare the steak.

2. Using paper towels, pat dry both sides of the steak. (This is essential to achieving a nice caramelization on the steak.) Drizzle both sides with olive oil and season evenly with salt and pepper.

3. Carefully remove skillet from the oven and place over medium-high heat on the stovetop for 2 minutes to keep it hot. When pan is piping hot, place steaks in skillet and cook, without moving, until a dark crust has formed on the bottom side, about 1 minute. Using tongs, flip steaks, and cook an additional 1 minute.

4. Place skillet in oven on the center rack (keep the oven on broil) and cook, flipping once, 3 to 5 minutes, until temperature registers 120 to 125 degrees F. for medium rare or 135 to 145 degrees F. for medium. Remove pan from oven, tent with foil, and rest 3 to 5 minutes. Serve immediately topped with a generous slice of garlic butter.

Braised Short Ribs

Our daughter Peyton has really taken a liking to cooking, baking, and photographing her creations. Braising meat is one of the easiest recipes because it's just a lot of baking, but it can feel overwhelming, especially to a kid. (See notes about braising on page 151.)

Prep: 30 min   *Cook:* 3 hours   *Total:* 3 hours 30 min   *Yield:* 4 servings

3 pounds beef short ribs

½ cup plus 1 tablespoon all-purpose flour, divided

1 teaspoon kosher salt

½ teaspoon ground black pepper

4 teaspoons olive oil, divided

3 tablespoons butter

⅓ cup minced onion

2 carrots, peeled and minced

2 stalks celery, minced

6 cloves garlic, minced

½ cup balsamic vinegar

1 tablespoon Worcestershire sauce

1 tablespoon liquid smoke

2 cups beef broth

2 sprigs fresh rosemary

4 sprigs fresh thyme

2 bay leaves

Prepared Mashed Potatoes (page 85)

Peyton Tip:
Start out by reading through the recipe and pulling ingredients out together. Chop, dice, mince, and arrange everything in little piles on a large cutting board or plate. Finally, start to prepare the recipe.

1. Preheat oven to 350 degrees F.

2. In a shallow bowl or pie tin, combine ½ cup flour, salt, and pepper. Coat each rib on all sides with flour mixture and set aside on platter or tray.

3. Heat 2 teaspoons oil in a Dutch oven or large oven-safe pot over medium-high heat until oil shimmers. Brown ribs 3 to 4 at a time on each side, then remove to a plate. Repeat until all ribs are browned. Wipe out any flour in the bottom of the pan, but leave all the browned bits.

4. Add butter and remaining 2 teaspoons oil to now-empty pot over medium heat. Quickly add onions, carrots, celery, and garlic and sauté 5 to 6 minutes, until veggies are tender. Add remaining 1 tablespoon flour and stir 30 seconds.

5. Stir in vinegar, Worcestershire sauce, liquid smoke, and beef broth. Bring to a simmer. Add herbs and bay leaves and arrange short ribs back in the pot.

6. Cover and cook 2 to 3 hours in preheated oven, until meat is falling off of bones. Remove bay leaves and herbs and serve hot over mashed potatoes.

Chocolate Cake   P 201

DESSERTS

Frozen Yogurt Bark

Every year—every day, really—I spend time trying to think of healthy snack ideas for my kids. And I'm so over it. I mean, how many times can you really eat an apple, string cheese, or veggies and dip? Fortunately, every now and then, I come up with something new. This healthy yogurt bark, packed with berries and topped with a chocolaty swirl, takes only a few minutes to make, and it gives the kids a chance to be creative as they think of new toppings to throw in the mix: coconut, bananas, granola, and so on. Simply spread the yogurt over a silicone mat and let the kids create something delicious.

Prep: **10 min**   *Freeze:* **4 hours**   *Total:* **4 hours 10 min**   *Yield:* **15 servings**

¾ cup semisweet chocolate chips

1 large (24-ounce) carton vanilla Greek yogurt

4 cups blackberries, blueberries, and raspberries

1. Place chocolate chips in a microwave-safe bowl. Heat in 30-second increments, stirring in between, until smooth. Set aside and allow to cool slightly.

2. Place a silicone mat on a rimmed baking sheet and spread the entire container of yogurt over the top. (If you don't own a silicone mat, you can use parchment paper, but you may get some resistance when trying to break up the frozen bark and separate it from the parchment.) Sprinkle berries over yogurt. Use a spoon to dot little mounds of chocolate all over the bark, and then use a toothpick to swirl the chocolate mounds.

3. Freeze at least 4 hours, until hardened, or overnight. Quickly break up the bark and store in an airtight container in the freezer up to 2 weeks.

Grayson Tip:
Sometimes the berries can fall off the bark, so I like to stir them into the yogurt and then spread it out. My sisters and I each make our own now. Peyton likes coconut, and Claire likes bananas. I always want sprinkles. It makes the yogurt look like a painting.

Monster Cookie Energy Bites

I take no credit for this recipe, and that feels really good. Kids' artworks or school projects can end up lost or in the trash, but a recipe created by a little one—that, I can make until my hands no longer move, and then he can make it for me and his children. It lasts forever.

I'm so proud of Grayson for making this recipe. These bites have become a really big deal in my house. All of us love them, and they can be made on the fly with whatever is in the pantry. As a bonus, they'll give you the energy needed to power through long days.

Time: 10 min   *Yield:* 30 energy bites

1½ cups old-fashioned rolled oats

2 tablespoons vanilla protein powder

1 cup creamy peanut butter

½ cup plus 1 tablespoon honey

⅓ cup raisins

⅓ cup mini chocolate chips

½ cup mini M&M's candies

½ teaspoon vanilla extract

1. Place all the ingredients in a large bowl and mix until everything is thoroughly combined.

2. Using a cookie scoop or clean hands, roll mixture into balls. Store in the refrigerator in an airtight container up to 2 weeks.

Grayson Tip:
Hide a few in the back of the fridge or your mom and dad will eat them while you're at school.

Rice Krispies Treats

Childhood is not complete until you've experienced real Rice Krispies Treats. Skip making them from the directions on the box, and instead do what our friend Kerri taught us: add salt and a dash of vanilla, then make them big, fluffy, and extra gooey.

Different salts are used for different things. Did you know you can use salt to amplify desserts? Most desserts should have salt (yes, even cookies). But what about on top? A bit of flaked sea salt on top of a Rice Krispies Treat or chocolate chip cookie adds this contrast of sweet and salty, a balance you didn't even know you were craving.

Time: **10 min**   *Yield:* **16 bars**

5 tablespoons butter

½ teaspoon fine sea salt

10 cups miniature marshmallows, divided

¼ teaspoon vanilla extract

6 cups Rice Krispies cereal

1. Spray a 9×9-inch pan with nonstick cooking spray and line it with foil or parchment paper. Spray again.
2. Place butter, salt, and 8 cups of the miniature marshmallows in a very large, microwave-safe bowl. Microwave on high power in 30-second increments, stirring in between, until everything is completely melted and smooth. Alternatively, use a large pot on the stovetop over medium heat and stir often until mixture is smooth and marshmallows and butter are thoroughly melted.
3. Add vanilla extract and stir to combine. Pour in Rice Krispies cereal and mix well. Stir in remaining marshmallows while mixture is still warm and then lightly press into prepared pan. To prevent sticking, grease a wooden spoon or rubber spatula with butter and use that to evenly press mixture into pan.
4. When mixture is set and cooled slightly, lift from pan with the foil or paper and cut into bars.

Claire Tip:
Have your mom watch for new cereal flavors. Last year I made strawberry Rice Krispies Treats, and they were so good.

Our Dessert Rule

One of the most important lessons I've learned about cooking is to seek moderation in all things. A balance is always required. As you learn to cook, you might find yourself pulled heavily toward certain foods, especially sweets. Because of that, our family enjoys dessert only one night a week. But when we do make it, watch out, because we know what's delicious and we aren't afraid to dig in!

Peach Crisp

Every year, my family went camping. Dad was a master at taking our little hands in his big ones and showing us all about fishing and hiking. Meanwhile, Mom made the best camp food ever. There was always one night during our camping adventure when, after our evening tradition of campfire songs, we'd get a Dutch oven peach dessert—the ultimate campfire food.

In the mountains I learned about family and love, but most of all, looking up at those gazillions of stars, I learned that Someone up there knew who I was, where I was, and whose I was.

This peach crisp is one of my favorites, a reminder of those moments, those people, and the perfection of fruit baked to golden deliciousness.

Prep: 20 min *Cook:* 40 min *Total:* 1 hour *Yield:* 8 to 10 servings

Filling

6 to 8 peaches, peeled and sliced (about 6 to 8 cups) (see sidebar)

2 tablespoons butter, melted

1 teaspoon ground cinnamon

¼ cup brown sugar

2 tablespoons cornstarch

Topping

¾ cup brown sugar

1 cup all-purpose flour

1½ cups old-fashioned rolled oats

½ teaspoon ground cinnamon

Pinch salt

¾ cup (1½ sticks) cold butter, cut into pieces

Vanilla ice cream, for serving

1. Preheat oven to 350 degrees F. Grease a 9x13-inch baking dish or a Dutch oven.

2. In a large bowl, toss peach slices with melted butter, cinnamon, ¼ cup brown

Peeling Peaches

Peaches can be hard to peel, but poaching peaches is easy. If the peach is underripe at all, or if you bought a variety that's known to not peel well, you may want to poach them:

1. Bring 3 quarts water to boil in a large pot.

2. Fill a large bowl with ice and 2 quarts water.

3. Use a paring knife to score a small x on the bottom of each peach.

4. When water is boiling, use a slotted spoon to gently place peaches in water. Boil 2 minutes, then remove peaches with slotted spoon and transfer to ice-cold water.

5. Let peaches sit in water 1 minute to stop cooking.

6. When cool enough to handle, use a paring knife and your thumb to grasp the skin at the x and pull the skin off.

If you are planning on baking the peaches for a dessert, it's best to avoid poaching, as it can break them down too fast. Instead, use a sharp paring knife, cut an x at the top of the peach, pinch the edge of the skin between your knife and thumb, and pull the skin down and off the peach.

Peyton Tip:

You can use canned peaches; just drain out the liquid. Also, sometimes we make the topping ahead of time and freeze it until we need it so we can make dessert in a hurry. Try all sorts of versions, like apple crisp or berry crisp.

sugar, and cornstarch. Arrange peaches over the bottom of prepared pan.

3. In a separate bowl, stir together ¾ cup brown sugar, flour, oats, cinnamon, and salt. Add butter pieces and use a pastry cutter or 2 forks to cut in butter until coarse crumbs form. Then use your hands to form mixture into a thick, almost paste-like texture.

4. Spread topping over fruit and bake 30 to 40 minutes, until filling is bubbly and top is crisp like a cookie. If topping is still soft, keep baking.

5. Cool 10 to 15 minutes before serving warm with a scoop of ice cream.

All Pans Are Not Created Equal

Glass pans give food a darker, crunchier crust, so they're generally best for casseroles, breads, and pies. Metal pans are perfect for absolutely everything, so other than a casserole dish for some main dishes, I pretty much bake only in metal pans. But here's the key: the darker the pan, the darker your baked goods will turn out. For that reason, I buy light metal pans and cookie sheets with a lip, also known as jelly roll pans.

THE GREAT FAMILY BAKEOFF

A few times a year, the five of us gather in the kitchen for a family bakeoff. The goal is for each of us to create a dish or treat that features one of five random main ingredients. I line the five ingredients up on the counter, put everyone's name in a hat, and then each person chooses an ingredient to work with when his or her name is picked. After every dish is made, we taste each creation and choose a winner.

In case you'd like to play, here are the rules of the game (to print off your own scorecards, visit our website at ohsweetbasil.com):

- Pick any recipe you'd like that starts with a basic main ingredient, like cookie dough, pizza dough, or even baked potatoes.

- Select one random ingredient for each person ahead of time and line them up on the counter (for cookies, think different mix-ins, for example).

- The person whose name is drawn first gets to pick an ingredient first. The person whose name is picked last ends up with whatever ingredient is left. Make sure all of the names get in the hat so that no one misses out.

- Everyone start baking! You must use your selected ingredient, but you can add anything else from the fridge or freezer. For example: Plain cookie dough was the main recipe, the random ingredient was frosted flakes cereal, and I added Craisins and chocolate chips to finish off my cookies.

- At the end, everyone can sample each dish— or dessert—and vote for their favorite.

- The winner gets all the glory and possibly gets to help pick the ingredients for next time.

Apple Dumplings

This recipe reminds me so much of my grandma's apple rolls recipe. Don't tell Grandma, but this is a much simpler version, one that still reminds me of her.

Grandma is so good at making every kid feel special. Any grandchild can run in and beg her to come see a special rock at the very back of the yard, and Grandma will bend down, look that little one right in the eyes, and take off hand in hand with the child to see it. It's easy to see where my mom got her patience. Some special gift was given to those two to see and love children, and every time I cook recipes like this one, I yearn to be like them.

Prep: 10 min *Cook:* 30 min *Total:* 40 min *Yield:* 16 dumplings

1 cup (2 sticks) salted butter

1 tablespoon granulated sugar mixed with ¼ teaspoon cinnamon

1 tablespoon all-purpose flour

2 Granny Smith or Honeycrisp apples, peeled, cored, and sliced into 8 pieces per apple

2 (8-ounce) cans refrigerated crescent rolls

1½ cups brown sugar

1 teaspoon vanilla extract

1½ teaspoons ground cinnamon

1 cup Sprite (see note)

Vanilla ice cream, for serving

1. Preheat oven to 350 degrees F. Liberally butter a 9x13-inch baking dish using part of the 1 cup butter called for in ingredients. Place remaining butter in a microwave-safe bowl and set aside.

2. Combine cinnamon-sugar mix and flour in large bowl, add apple slices, and toss to coat.

3. On a lightly floured countertop, pat out each crescent roll to increase the size just a little. Roll each apple slice in a crescent roll and place in prepared baking dish.

4. In the microwave, melt butter that was set aside in step 1. Stir in brown sugar, vanilla extract, and cinnamon. Pour melted-butter mixture over the tops of all the dumplings. Pour Sprite along the edges of the pan and in between the rolls but not over the rolls.

5. Bake 30 to 35 minutes, until golden brown on top. Serve warm with a scoop of ice cream, if desired.

NOTE: We prefer the flavor of Sprite for this recipe, but you can also use 7UP or a generic lemon-lime soda.

No Bake Oreo Pie

Are you a dipper, a dunker, a twister, or a cruncher?

You know what I'm talking about. Some Oreo eaters do a little dip; some dunk and hold the cookie in the milk (that's me); some twist it open and eat out the middle (who are you hooligans?!); and finally, some just chomp right into it.

Oreos are a classic dessert that you think you've risen above until it's in front of you, and then you just can't resist. Who needs the crème brûlée, I want the cookie of my childhood! Starting your pie making with a no-bake pie will help you to feel confident with creating a crust and filling, pulling out the perfect slice, and watching everyone applaud you for it.

Prep: 15 min   *Optional Cook:* 10 min   *Chill:* 1 hour
Total: 1 hour 15 min to 1 hour 25 min   *Yield:* 8 servings

Crust

10 chocolate graham crackers

¼ cup granulated sugar

¼ cup butter, melted

Filling

⅔ cup milk

⅓ cup chocolate milk

1 (4.2-ounce) package Jell-O Instant Oreo Cookies 'n Cream Pudding and Pie Filling (see note)

4 ounces cream cheese, softened

½ cup sweetened condensed milk

1½ cups nondairy whipped topping, such as Cool Whip, thawed and divided (see note)

Garnish

1 sleeve Oreo cookies, crushed

1 cup fresh whipped cream, for topping (see note)

1. Prepare crust: In a food processor, crush chocolate graham crackers into fine crumbs, using 10 to 12 one-second pulses. Add sugar and pulse several times to combine. Transfer to a bowl and stir in melted butter. Press mixture into a 9-inch pie dish and chill in refrigerator 30 minutes. Alternatively, you can bake the crust in a 375-degree oven 10 minutes.

2. Prepare filling: In a large bowl, whisk together milk, chocolate milk, and pudding mix. Set aside. In a separate, large bowl, beat the cream cheese with an electric mixer until smooth. Add sweetened

Pro Tip: To serve pie, make cuts for three pieces, but remove the center piece first. Having both sides loosened up will allow that first piece to come out with ease.

No Bake Oreo Pie *(continued)*

condensed milk and beat again until smooth. Add pudding to the cream cheese mixture and stir until evenly combined. Gently fold in ⅓ of the whipped topping. Once combined, add remaining whipped topping a little at a time. (Adding the whipped topping a little at a time makes for a lighter, fluffier filling.) Spread filling evenly into prepared crust and chill 30 to 60 minutes in the refrigerator.

3. Just before serving, sprinkle top of pie generously with crushed Oreo cookies. Then, when serving, top each slice with a generous dollop of fresh whipped cream.

Pie will keep 2 to 3 days covered loosely with plastic wrap and stored in refrigerator.

NOTE: If you can't find Oreo pudding, just use French vanilla or cheesecake pudding and add in one sleeve of crushed Oreos.

NOTE: You can use fresh whipped cream in place of the nondairy whipped topping. To yield enough fresh whipped cream for both the filling and topping, use an electric mixer on high speed to beat 1½ cups heavy cream with 2½ to 3 tablespoons sugar until stiff peaks form. This will yield about 3 cups fresh whipped cream.

FOR THE LAST TIME

I once read a quote that said something like this: "At some point in your childhood, you and your friends went outside to play together for the last time, and none of you knew it."

After I read it, I sat for a while with a throbbing heart, thinking, *This is so true. They don't even know that their childhood is slipping away.*

And then it hit me.

At some point as a mother, I held them for the last time. And neither of us even knew it.

That's why some days we don't cook or clean. Instead we have smoothies for dinner, then we snuggle up on the couch, everyone so close together it's almost uncomfortable. After all, it might be the last time we get to do this.

Life is meant to be lived. Whether you're getting ready to head into fifth grade or go off to college next year, or you're the mom sitting with your legs pulled up under you and tearing up at the thought of your babies no longer needing you, you will never forget a spontaneous night of making cookies and dancing to music turned up a little too high.

Food connects more than just people and memories; it connects hearts.

Wouldn't it be kind of amazing if we could recognize the moment a food memory is being made—while it's happening?

I've been trying to do this a lot lately: grabbing chubby cheeks and saying, "Today is a good day," then giving a little wink and a smile as we run off to surprise the neighbors with a water-gun fight.

Cherry Pie Bars

There are a lot of classic desserts I grew up with in the eighties and nineties that just don't show up much anymore: yellow cake with chocolate frosting, anyone? It's super tempting to get sucked into Pinterest and make only new recipes. But I'm a big believer in keeping a recipe from your childhood alive. This one actually is not mine, but so many of you reached out to share this one that I wanted to give a little nod to the people who are remembering their own kitchen time with friends and family. I'm just really grateful for so many of you who are trying to live a happy and delicious life and have invited our little family into your kitchens.

Prep: **15 min** *Cook:* **30 min** *Cool:* **2 hours** *Total:* **2 hours 45 min** *Yield:* **26 bars**

Crust and Topping

1 cup (2 sticks) unsalted butter, softened

2 cups granulated sugar

1½ teaspoons vanilla extract, divided

½ teaspoon almond extract

4 large eggs

½ teaspoon salt

3 cups all-purpose flour

Filling

2 (21-ounce) cans cherry pie filling

Zest of 1 lemon

¼ teaspoon ground cinnamon

Drizzle

1 cup powdered sugar

2 tablespoons milk

1. Preheat oven to 350 degrees F. Grease a 12x17-inch rimmed jelly roll pan.
2. In the bowl of a stand mixer fitted with the paddle attachment, cream together butter and granulated sugar until smooth, about 2 minutes. Add 1 teaspoon vanilla extract, almond extract, and eggs and mix again until smooth. On low speed, mix in salt and 2 cups of the flour until almost combined. Add remaining 1 cup flour and mix well. Carefully spread 3 cups of the dough over bottom of prepared pan.
3. In a large bowl, stir together pie filling, lemon zest, and cinnamon.
4. Pour filling evenly over crust. Using a tablespoon, drop dollops of remaining dough all over the top of the filling.
5. Bake 25 to 30 minutes, until top is golden brown and filling is bubbly. Cool completely on a wire rack.
6. Once cool, whisk together powdered sugar, milk, and remaining ½ teaspoon vanilla in a small bowl. Drizzle all over cooled bars, cut, and serve.

Carmelitas

I love switching up desserts. Don't get me wrong: chocolate chip cookies and brownies are great, but occasionally my sweet tooth gets restless and wants something special.

The tops and bottoms of these Carmelitas are like an oatmeal crisp. Sandwiched in between is a gooey layer of chocolate and caramel. Each bite gives you something gooey, melty, and crispy—it is divine!

This recipe is so easy to make, and it's perfect for when you want a little something sweet but aren't up for a huge kitchen project. Plus, it's the perfect opportunity to get the kids in the kitchen to help.

Prep: 20 min   *Cook:* 25 min   *Total:* 45 min   *Yield:* 21 to 24 bars

Crust and Topping

2 cups all-purpose flour

2 cups old-fashioned rolled oats

¼ teaspoon salt

2 teaspoons baking soda

2 cups firmly packed brown sugar

1⅓ cups butter, melted

Filling

1½ (11-ounce) bags Kraft Caramels, unwrapped

½ cup evaporated milk

¼ cup heavy cream

1 cup milk chocolate chips

1 cup semisweet chocolate chips

1. Preheat oven to 350 degrees F. Line a 9x13-inch baking pan with parchment paper or aluminum foil, leaving a 2-inch overhang on each side for easy lifting later. Spray paper or foil with nonstick cooking spray. (You can use a smaller pan but will end up with thicker, and fewer, bars.)

2. In a large bowl, mix together flour, oats, salt, baking soda, brown sugar, and melted butter until combined well. Sprinkle half of the mixture in prepared pan, pressing down to cover the bottom, and bake 10 minutes. When 10 minutes are up, remove from oven but do not turn off oven.

3. While oat mixture bakes, place unwrapped caramels, evaporated milk, and cream in a saucepan over low heat. Stir frequently until caramels are melted and mixture is thoroughly combined.

4. Sprinkle chocolate chips over baked mixture and then pour melted caramel evenly over the chips. Sprinkle remaining oat mixture over caramel and bake 15 minutes.

5. Let cool completely in pan on wire rack. Use parchment paper to lift out of pan and cut into bars when ready to serve.

MAKING COOKIES WITH DAD

I would give just about anything in the world for a picture of my dad and me when I was four years old, making oatmeal raisin chocolate chip cookies together.

I can still feel myself sitting up on the counter, my feet dangling over the side, kicking my heels against the counter, tap, tap, tip tap, as we dumped ingredient after ingredient into the mixer bowl.

Now Dad is the best grandpa to do anything with—he acts just like the dad he was. No matter what he was doing (and cue my tears, who knew cookies would choke me up so much?!), Dad would bring us along, explaining and letting us feel, fix, paint, or whatever right alongside him. He made us feel like he absolutely needed our expertise and help. "Ahhh, see how it's getting tighter?" he would say. "Sing, 'leftie loosie, rightie tightie,' and you'll always get it right."

That little phrase still goes through my head today.

There he was, pulling the beater off of the mixer, and I was all googly-eyed over the cookie dough when suddenly he stuck it right in my hands. "How do you know if it's going to be good if you don't test it?" And I sat there, licking the beater as fast as I could, and no, I didn't die from raw cookie dough, but man, if that's the way I have to go . . .

Dad didn't cook very much, but there are a few really important things I learned about cooking from him:

1. Always cook with your kids. Food feels safe, so so your conversations and relationships end up feeling safe too. Barriers drop and hearts end up mixed together better than any dough you'll ever make.

2. Be present. It takes only 10 minutes to really connect. He was probably busy at work the rest of the day, but all I remember is having his undivided attention for cookies. When at work, be at work; when at home, be home; and try really hard to be home more than work.

3. Always eat some of the cookie dough and the first cookie out of the oven.

Chocolate Chip Cookies

You stick one of these chocolate chip cookies in front of me and I'm diving in ASAP, no waiting until the next day for me!

Prep: 10 min *Cook:* 10 min *Total:* 20 min *Yield:* 24 cookies

1¾ cups plus 2 tablespoons all-purpose flour

¾ teaspoon salt

1 teaspoon baking soda

½ teaspoon cornstarch

1¼ cups unsalted butter, at room temperature (see note)

1 cup brown sugar

½ cup granulated sugar

2 large eggs

2 teaspoons vanilla extract

1½ to 2 cups semisweet chocolate chips

1. Preheat oven to 375 degrees F. Line baking sheets with parchment paper or silicone mats.
2. In a medium bowl, whisk together flour, salt, baking soda, and cornstarch; set aside.
3. In the bowl of a stand mixer fitted with the paddle attachment, cream together butter, brown sugar, and granulated sugar on medium-high speed until light and fluffy, about 2 minutes. Add eggs and vanilla and mix to combine.
4. Add flour mixture and mix on low speed until almost fully incorporated. Add chocolate chips and mix to combine.
5. With your hands or a cookie scoop, scoop out a golf ball–sized amount of dough and roll into ball. Place cookie dough balls 2 inches apart on prepared cookie sheet.
6. Bake 8 to 10 minutes, until tops are golden in a few places and bottoms look set. Tops should not be brown. Cool on pan 2 minutes before transferring to wire cooling racks.

NOTE: You don't want your butter to be too soft for this recipe. When it's room temperature, you should be able to press down on the stick with your thumb and leave a nice thumbprint but not have your thumb sink through the butter.

Grayson Tip:
We often scoop the cookie dough into balls and place them a freezer bag. That way, we can bake some up anytime straight from the freezer.

Chocolate Chip Cookie Variations

We decided to share some family bakeoff winners with you! We used our chocolate chip cookie recipe, and each person created a cookie with their secret ingredient.

S'mores Chocolate Chip Cookies

1 recipe chocolate chip cookie dough (page 189)

4 whole graham crackers, each split into 2 halves

4 Hershey's milk chocolate bars, each split into 2 halves

8 marshmallows

1. Follow instructions for chocolate chip cookies through step 4.

2. With your hands or an extra-large cookie scoop, scoop out ¼ cup dough and roll into a ball. With your hands, flatten ball into a disc shape.

3. Cut a marshmallow in half, placing both halves side by side on a graham cracker, and top with a chocolate piece. Place on top of the disc of dough.

4. Top with another flat piece of cookie dough and seal the edges to make a s'mores cookie sandwich. Repeat with remaining ingredients to make 8 sandwiches total.

5. Chill in refrigerator 15 minutes, then bake 3 cookies at a time on a cookie sheet 16 to 18 minutes, until golden on top.

Cookies and Cream Cookies

1 recipe chocolate chip cookie dough (page 189)

4 Hershey's Cookies 'N' Creme bars or Twix Cookies & Cream bars

Make chocolate chip cookies as directed, but instead of chocolate chips, mix in 4 Hershey's Cookies 'N' Creme bars or Twix Cookies & Cream bars, chopped (about 1½ to 2 cups).

S'mores   Cookies and Cream   Craisin Frosted Flakes

Craisin Frosted Flakes Cookies

1 recipe chocolate chip cookie dough
   (page 189)

1 cup mini chocolate chips

1 cup Craisins, chopped

1 cup Frosted Flakes cereal

1. Follow instructions for chocolate chip cookies through step 3.
2. Add flour mixture and mix on low speed until almost fully incorporated, then add the chocolate chips, Craisins, and Frosted Flakes.
3. Scoop cookies by using a cookie scoop, but do not scrape against the side of the bowl; merely scoop, lift, and round the bottom with the other hand. Place dough balls on cookie sheet 2 inches apart.
4. Bake 8 to 10 minutes, until bottoms look set but tops are not yet brown, just golden in some places. Allow to cool for 2 minutes before moving to a cooling rack or into your mouth.

Lemon Drop Cookies

Carrian: This is a cookie that made Peyton and me get into a little scuffle. Sometimes it's hard to not step in as a parent.

Peyton: Yeah, and sometimes it's really hard if your mom is ALWAYS stepping in. ☺

Carrian: Maybe I can get a bit fussy in the kitchen, but Peyton did awesome. So, Peyton, take the glory . . .

Peyton: These Lemon Drop Cookies are my new favorite. I know you might doubt me, but TRY THIS COOKIE, then thank me for making my mom let me have control of the kitchen. I see her rolling her eyes—gee, Mom, wonder who I get that habit from, haha!

Carrian: I now keep lemon drops on hand, and yes, we kind of adore each other. She's the best.

Prep: 15 min   *Cook:* 12 min   *Total:* 27 min   *Yield:* 4 to 5 dozen cookies

---

4 cups all-purpose flour

1½ teaspoons baking soda

1½ teaspoons baking powder

1 teaspoon salt

2 cups granulated sugar

1½ cups shortening

3 large eggs

1 teaspoon vanilla extract

1 teaspoon lemon extract

Zest of 1 lemon

1 (9-ounce) bag Brach's Lemon Drops, crushed in blender (about ¾ cup when crushed)

3 cups powdered sugar

Juice of 2 lemons, about ¼ cup

1. Preheat oven to 350 degrees F. Line baking sheets with parchment paper or silicone mats.

2. In a medium bowl, whisk together flour, baking soda, baking powder, and salt; set aside.

3. In the bowl of a stand mixer fitted with the paddle attachment, cream together sugar, shortening, and eggs. Mix in vanilla extract and lemon extract.

4. Add flour mixture, followed by lemon zest and crushed lemon drops, mixing well to combine.

5. Scoop out golf ball–sized amounts of dough and roll into balls.

6. Arrange balls 2 inches apart on prepared baking sheet and slightly flatten each ball with the palm of your hand or the bottom of a drinking glass that has been dipped in flour. Bake 10 to 12 minutes, until light and fluffy and the tops are beginning to look a little dry, but not browned at all.

7. Let cookies cool 2 minutes on pan, then transfer to wire racks.

8. In a small bowl, whisk together powdered sugar and lemon juice until smooth. Brush generously over cookie tops and let cookies cool completely before serving.

Sugar Cookies

I have spent years searching for how to make cutout sugar cookies that are still soft and delicious. This recipe is the grand prize winner, and I'm a stitch embarrassed over where it comes from.

I remember my mom making sugar cookies with me a few times growing up, but I don't remember loving them. So when she learned I was testing recipes and texted me to ask, "Why don't you try my recipe?" I was skeptical. But then I remembered that she had always rolled her cookies out thin. So I tried her recipe, rolling them out all thick and chewy like a good baker should, and sure enough, they're PERFECT!

Prep: 15 min *Chill:* 10 min *Cook:* 8 min *Total:* 33 min *Yield:* About 24 cookies

---

3 cups all-purpose flour

1½ teaspoons baking powder

¼ teaspoon salt

1 cup unsalted butter, softened

1 cup granulated sugar

1 large egg

½ teaspoon vanilla extract

¾ teaspoon almond extract

1 to 2 tablespoons heavy cream (optional)

Sugar Cookie Icing (page 196)

1. Preheat oven to 350 degrees F. Line baking sheets with parchment paper or silicone baking mats.

2. In a medium bowl, whisk together flour, baking powder, and salt; set aside.

3. In the bowl of a stand mixer fitted with the paddle attachment, beat together butter and sugar until light and fluffy, 1½ to 2 minutes. Add egg, vanilla extract, and almond extract and beat again. Slowly mix in flour mixture until combined. Dough will be soft and crumbly, but it will come together as you grab it and shape it into a ball. (If not, add a little cream here.) Wrap dough tightly in plastic wrap and chill in refrigerator 10 minutes. You can make the dough well ahead of time if you'd like. Just make sure if it chills more than 10 to 20 minutes that it rests on the counter 10 minutes or so before rolling out.

4. Lightly dust work surface with powdered sugar and roll out dough to ¼- to ½-inch thick. Cut into shapes with cookie cutters and place on prepared baking sheets 1 inch apart. Continue cutting shapes as close together as possible and rerolling scraps as needed until all dough is

Grayson Tip:
Roll cookies out in powdered sugar instead of flour because it doesn't make them dry and, when you try stealing some and licking it, it won't taste yucky like flour.

used. Try to avoid working the dough too much; just get those cookie cutters close together.

5. Bake 7 to 8 minutes for soft cookies. Cookies will not brown. If you like crispier cookies, bake 1 to 2 minutes more, until edges begin to brown slightly. Transfer cookies to wire racks and cool completely.

6. To frost, use a small piping bag or plastic bag with one corner barely cut off, or squeeze bottles are great for kids, and carefully design your cookies.

Sugar Cookie Icing

Time: **5 min**

3 cups powdered sugar

4 tablespoons milk

2 tablespoons light corn syrup

½ teaspoon vanilla extract

Food coloring of choice

In a large bowl, using a wooden spoon or whisk, mix together powdered sugar, milk, corn syrup, and vanilla until smooth and shiny. Add a few drops food coloring and mix again.

IT'S GOING TO BE A CAKEWALK

- Use a baking spray made specifically for cakes as well as a parchment round in the bottom of the pan to help the cake release more easily.

- Espresso powder and hot water can be used in place of coffee in recipes that call for it. Espresso powder also enhances chocolate flavors, and sometimes, all you need is a teaspoon. Many stores carry espresso powder in the baking section. You can also find it online.

- Do not overmix your cake batter. It's easy to become hypnotized by the swirling and mixing as the batter comes together, but don't succumb to it. Turn the mixer off when it's time.

- Use a toothpick inserted at the center to tell if a cake is done. If it comes out clean, it's done. You can also gently press down on the cake with your index and middle fingers; if it bounces back, it's done. If your fingers leave a dent, bake it a little longer.

- Allow cakes to cool completely before removing them from a pan or turning them out onto a cooling rack. This will also help prevent a cake from crumbling when you slice it.

- Level the cakes by removing the dome on top if there is one.

- For best storage, slice cake into pieces and wrap each piece in plastic wrap.

Banana Bundt Cake

This is one of my new favorite desserts, and I think it's because of how moist the actual cake turns out. It's great with or without the cream cheese frosting.

Prep: 10 min   *Cook:* 35 min   *Total:* 45 min   *Yield:* 12 servings

---

1 (15.25-ounce) box yellow cake mix (see note)

1 (3.4-ounce) package Jell-O Banana Cream Instant Pudding

4 large eggs, lightly beaten

1 cup water

3 tablespoons sour cream

¼ cup canola oil

2 overripe bananas, mashed (about 1 cup)

1. Adjust oven rack to lower-middle position and preheat oven to 350 degrees F. Grease and flour a 10-inch nonstick Bundt pan and set aside.

2. In a large bowl, whisk together dry cake mix and instant pudding mix. Add eggs, water, sour cream, and oil. Whisk until just incorporated. Using a rubber spatula, fold in mashed bananas until just combined; do not overmix.

3. Pour batter into prepared Bundt pan. Shake pan slightly to even out the batter. Bake 35 to 45 minutes, until top is a light golden color and a toothpick inserted in center comes out with only a few crumbs attached.

4. Let cake cool in pan on a cooling rack. Once cool, use a knife to loosen cake from pan's sides. Invert and remove cake to a platter.

5. If desired, drizzle Simple Cream Cheese Frosting with a large spoon held over the top of the cake.

Simple Cream Cheese Frosting

4 ounces cream cheese, softened

1½ cups powdered sugar

½ teaspoon vanilla extract

1 teaspoon heavy cream, up to 2 tablespoons as needed

In a large bowl, whip cream cheese with an electric mixer until smooth, about 2 minutes. Beat in powdered sugar, then add vanilla and heavy cream. Adjust amount of cream for a thinner frosting, if desired.

NOTE: Although we prefer yellow cake mix in this recipe, a white or butter cake mix can be used in its place. Heck, even a chocolate cake mix would be awesome!

Chocolate Cake

Not long ago, I had a cake for my birthday for the first time since I was a little girl. Gasp! (I'm a big pie fan.) I felt like it was time to get back to the beauty of birthdays, and for me that involves a big, fat three-layer chocolate cake.

Plus, we were in quarantine. Remember that? So much quality time. There were a few days I even made the kids abide by social distancing FROM ME. KIDS, I NEED 6 FEET!

So listen, blah blah blah, I love my kids and think they are the best in all the land, but I'm also realistic, and sometimes Mommy needs a break, and it had better include a closet, no whining children, and a slice of this cake.

Prep: 20 min *Cook:* 35 min *Cool:* 2 hours *Total:* 2 hours 55 min *Yield:* 16 slices

3 cups all-purpose flour

3 cups granulated sugar

1½ cups unsweetened cocoa powder

1 tablespoon baking soda

1½ teaspoons baking powder

1½ teaspoons salt

4 large eggs, at room temperature (see note)

1½ cups buttermilk (see note)

1½ cups warm water

1 teaspoon baking espresso powder (see note)

½ cup vegetable oil

1 tablespoon vanilla extract

Chocolate Cream Cheese Frosting (page 202)

1. Preheat oven to 350 degrees F. Grease and flour three 9-inch round cake pans.

2. In a large bowl, whisk together flour, sugar, cocoa powder, baking soda, baking powder, and salt; set aside. In the bowl of a stand mixer fitted with the paddle attachment, combine eggs, buttermilk, warm water, espresso powder, oil, and vanilla and mix on medium speed until combined. Add the dry ingredients and mix until smooth.

3. Divide batter evenly between the three prepared pans. (Each pan will hold 3 heaping cups batter.) Bake 30 to 35 minutes, until a toothpick inserted in center comes out clean.

4. Cool in pans on wire racks 20 minutes, then turn out to cool completely.

5. If one cake is more rounded, use a serrated knife to level it flat. Put the crumb side down when frosting. Separate the frosting into 3 parts, leaving the third part bigger than the others as you need it to cover the whole cake.

6. Place a cake layer on a stand and top with chocolate frosting, spreading with an offset spatula; do not worry about the sides yet. Add another layer and do the same. Add the

Chocolate Cake *(continued)*

final layer and the rest of the frosting and smooth it down the sides and over the top, making whatever design you prefer.

NOTE: This recipe turns out best when all ingredients are the same temperature, hence the directions for eggs and buttermilk to be at room temperature. Ideally, set them out on the counter 30 to 40 minutes before prepping the recipe. If you forget, 10 minutes should be sufficient.

NOTE: Espresso powder can be found in the baking aisle, but you can also use real espresso if you prefer.

Chocolate Cream Cheese Frosting

Time: 10 min   *Yield:* about 6 cups

1 cup unsalted butter, softened

12 ounces cream cheese, softened

Pinch salt

1¼ cups unsweetened cocoa powder

7 to 8 cups powdered sugar

2 teaspoons vanilla extract

1 to 2 tablespoons whole milk, plus more if needed

In the bowl of a stand mixer fitted with the paddle attachment (or in a large bowl with an electric hand mixer), beat butter and cream cheese until fluffy, 2 to 3 minutes. Add pinch of salt, cocoa powder, powdered sugar, and vanilla and mix on low until combined. Once combined, increase speed and beat until smooth, adding milk a tablespoon at a time until mixture is spreadable.

Nutella-Stuffed Cupcakes

Claire: One day, I convinced my mom to let me try making a Nutella cupcake. The secret, I learned, was that if I clean up, I get to bake all the time. I used one of her chocolate cake recipes, and she taught me how to frost cupcakes for the first time. This picture is of the cupcake I made and frosted myself.

Prep: 1 hour *Cook:* 17 min *Cool:* 1 hour
Total: 2 hours 17 min *Yield:* 18 to 24 cupcakes

8 ounces semisweet chocolate, finely chopped

⅔ cup Dutch-process cocoa powder

4 teaspoons espresso powder

1½ cups very hot water

1½ cups cake flour

1½ cups granulated sugar

1 teaspoon salt

1 teaspoon baking soda

¾ cup canola oil or vegetable oil

4 large eggs, at room temperature

4 teaspoons white vinegar

1 teaspoon vanilla extract

⅔ cup Nutella

Strawberry Buttercream (page 205)

1. Preheat oven to 350 degrees F. Line 2 standard 12-cup muffin tins with foil or paper liners.

2. Place chopped chocolate and cocoa powder in a medium glass bowl and set aside. In a liquid measuring cup, stir espresso powder into hot water until combined. Pour over chocolate and cocoa powder, whisking gently until chocolate is smooth and melted. Cover with plastic wrap and set aside to cool completely.

3. In a small bowl, whisk together flour, sugar, salt, and baking soda; set aside. In a separate bowl, whisk together the oil, eggs, vinegar, and vanilla. Pour oil mixture into cooled chocolate mixture and stir with a wooden spoon until smooth. Pour chocolate mixture into flour mixture, stirring until smooth. Using a cookie scoop, divide batter evenly among prepared muffin cups, filling each ¾ full.

4. Bake until cupcakes are set and tops are firm and bounce back when pressed, 17 to 19 minutes. Remove from oven and cool completely, at least 1 hour.

5. When completely cooled, use an apple corer or paring knife to slice a small section out of the center of each cupcake. Make sure not to pierce the bottom of the cupcake. Fill each hole with 1 heaping

Peyton and Claire Tip: We love doing cupcake wars together to see who frosts best.

Start frosting from the center of the cupcake, working your way outward to the edge, then lift straight up to end the frosting.

Nutella-Stuffed Cupcakes (continued)

spoonful Nutella. Pop the very top of the removed cupcake core back onto each cupcake before frosting.

6. Spoon Strawberry Buttercream into a piping bag fitted with a decorative tip, such as a Wilton 1M piping tip, pipe frosting on cupcakes, and serve.

Strawberry Buttercream

Time: 10 minutes   *Yield:* 4 to 5 cups

2 cups unsalted butter, at room
   temperature

1 teaspoon vanilla extract

⅔ cup seedless strawberry jam

6 cups powdered sugar, sifted

In the bowl of stand mixer fitted with the whisk attachment, beat butter on medium-high speed until smooth, about 1 minute. Add vanilla and strawberry jam and beat to combine, about 30 seconds. Add powdered sugar, 1 cup at a time, beating well on medium speed after each addition. Continue beating 4 to 5 minutes, until light and fluffy.

Mini Twix Cheesecakes

When we decided to develop a new mini-cheesecake recipe, we wanted to make it both easy and delicious. It took a little bit of work, but I think we did it.

These Mini Twix Cheesecakes are the easiest cheesecakes ever. You don't need a water bath, a long list of ingredients, or even much time. In fact, the majority of the "cooking time" is actually just chilling time in the fridge.

Prep: 20 min   *Cook:* 15 min   *Chill:* 2 hours
Total: 2 hours 35 min   *Yield:* 12 mini cheesecakes

Pro Tip: Over-beating incorporates too much air, which leads to cracking and splitting on the top of the cheesecake.

Incorporate eggs one at a time so that they are completely mixed in and cannot cause any separation in baking.

Kids' Tip:
Mom loves Twix bars, but this recipe is also delicious with Reese's Peanut Butter Cups, swirls of caramel, or berries.

Crust

9 whole graham crackers

4 tablespoons butter, melted

⅓ cup plus 1 teaspoon granulated sugar, divided

Filling

2 (8-ounce) packages cream cheese, softened

1 teaspoon vanilla extract

2 large eggs

1 cup halved Twix Caramel Bites Chocolate Cookie candies, divided

¼ cup caramel sauce

1. Preheat oven to 350 degrees F. Line a standard 12-cup muffin tin with paper or foil liners.
2. In a medium bowl, stir together graham cracker crumbs, butter, and 1 teaspoon sugar. Portion crumbs into prepared muffin tin, using a spoon to press down mixture. Bake 5 minutes, then remove and set aside.
3. In a large bowl, beat cream cheese with an electric hand mixer until smooth and creamy, about 2 minutes. Add remaining ⅓ cup sugar and vanilla extract and beat again.
4. Add eggs, one at a time, beating on low speed until just incorporated.
5. Gently fold ½ cup of the Twix Bites into the batter. Divide batter evenly between the cupcake liners. Drizzle a little caramel over each and then use a toothpick to swirl caramel into batter. Sprinkle as many remaining Twix Bites as you'd like over each top.
6. Bake 15 to 16 minutes, until set. Cool on a wire rack to room temperature, then chill in refrigerator 1 to 2 hours.

Strawberry Pie

Strawberry shortcake is my absolute favorite summer dessert, right below marionberry pie. But here's the deal, if you're going to learn to cook and bake, you HAVE to have a pie recipe. So here was my issue: if I added strawberry shortcake in here, then wouldn't a strawberry pie be too much? So which should I choose?

Finally the pie won because

1. You'll learn to make a pie crust.
2. You'll learn how to make stabilized whipped cream, which is the secret to a perfectly decorated, non-weeping pie.
3. The filling is so simple you won't be overwhelmed with steps.
4. It's technically the best of my two favorite desserts in one: strawberries and pie!

Prep: 30 min   *Chill:* 3 hours   *Total:* 3 hours 30 minutes   *Yield:* 8 servings

2 cups water

2 cups granulated sugar

6 tablespoons cornstarch

Zest of 1 lemon

1 (6-ounce) package strawberry-flavored gelatin

3 pounds fresh strawberries, washed and hulled

1 baked and cooled 9-inch pie shell (see note), such as our No-Fail Homemade Pie Crust (page 211)

1½ cups Stabilized Whipped Cream (page 210)

1. In a medium saucepan over high heat, bring water, sugar, and cornstarch to a boil. Stir continuously, until thick and clear, about 5 minutes. Remove from heat and vigorously stir in lemon zest and strawberry gelatin, mixing until gelatin is thoroughly dissolved, 2 to 3 minutes. Transfer to a large bowl to cool for 10 minutes.

2. Fold whole, hulled strawberries into gelatin mixture and coat well.

3. Pour filling in baked and cooled pie shell and refrigerate until set, about 3 hours. (The finished pie can be made up to 24 hours in advance and chilled in refrigerator until ready to serve.)

4. Just before serving, spoon Stabilized Whipped Cream into a piping bag fitted with a Wilton 1M piping tip and pipe around edges of pie.

NOTE: Pie crust should be completely cooled before pouring in filling.

Stabilized Whipping Cream

Prep: 5 min   *Yield:* 1½ cups stabilized whipping cream

¼ teaspoon unflavored powdered
gelatin

¾ tablespoon water

¾ cup heavy cream, chilled

1 teaspoon granulated sugar

¼ teaspoon vanilla extract, or to taste

1. Sprinkle unflavored powdered gelatin over water in a microwave-safe bowl. Let stand
3 minutes, then microwave on high power in 1 or 2 five-second increments until gelatin
is dissolved and liquefied. Stir briefly and set aside to cool.

2. In the bowl of a stand mixer fitted with the whisk attachment, whip chilled heavy
cream, sugar, and vanilla on low speed until small bubbles form. Increase speed to medium and beat until soft peaks form (cream is thickened somewhat, and whisk leaves
a trail when lifted or moved around). With mixer still running, slowly pour in the gelatin
mixture, increase speed to high, and beat until stiff peaks form (the cream will stay
straight up when whisk lifts it up), about 1 minute.

3. Use as desired in any recipe that calls for whipped cream. Store in refrigerator if not
using immediately. Can be made up to 24 hours in advance.

No-Fail Homemade Pie Crust

Prep: **15 min**   *Cook:* **20 min**   *Total:* **35 min**
Yield: **Pastry for 1 double-crust pie or 2 (9-inch) pies**

3 cups all-purpose flour

1 teaspoon salt

1¼ cups shortening, chilled

1 large egg

1 tablespoon white vinegar

½ cup ice-cold water (see note)

1. In large bowl, whisk together flour and salt. With a pastry cutter or two forks, work shortening into flour 3 to 4 minutes, until mixture resembles coarse crumbs.
2. In a small bowl, beat egg with a fork. Add vinegar and mix until well combined. Stir in water.
3. Pour wet ingredients into flour mixture and stir with a fork until dough comes together.
4. Divide dough in half and shape each half into a 4-inch disc. For use with double-crust pies, follow directions in specific recipe.
5. For a single-crust pie, heat oven to 375 degrees F. Wrap one dough disc tightly in plastic wrap and place in a freezer bag. Seal bag and freeze for future use. (When ready to use, thaw in refrigerator overnight, then roll out as described in step 6.)
6. On a well-floured surface, roll out dough to a 12-inch circle. Transfer dough to a 9-inch pie dish, leaving an overhang around the edges. (With this particular recipe, I've found that it works well when transferring dough to pie plate to fold the dough in half and then in half again. Move folded dough to pie plate and unfold in center of pan.) Trim overhang to a uniform ½ inch around edges. Fold overhang under itself so it is flush with edge of pie plate. Flute as desired.
7. Pierce dough all over with tines of a fork and bake 15 to 20 minutes, until light golden brown.

NOTE: It's important that the water be ice-cold. I usually fill a bowl with water and add a handful of ice cubes before starting the recipe. Then, when the recipe calls for water, I remove the ice cubes and measure out ½ cup water from the bowl.

Raspberry Sweet Rolls

My mom and dad have rows and rows of raspberry bushes, and every summer we head out to Rexburg, Idaho, to help pick raspberries. The kids are pros at fighting through tangled branches to gather every single plump berry. Our motto is "one for the bucket, one for me." The kids love to feel so proud of all they picked, but mostly they want Grandma to make these easy raspberry sweet rolls.

Picture soft and fluffy dough filled with beautiful, fresh, slightly sweetened raspberries, baked until golden, and topped with a flawless frosting. Is your mouth watering?

A good recipe is all about balance, so don't be tempted with the "if some is good, more is better!" idea and slop on the frosting.

Prep: 20 min *Rest:* 3 hours *Cook:* 30 min
Total: 3 hours 50 min *Yield:* 12 sweet rolls

Dough

1 cup whole milk

3 tablespoons unsalted butter, cut into 3 pieces

¼ cup granulated sugar

2¼ teaspoons instant yeast

1 large egg, beaten

2½ to 3 cups all-purpose flour

1½ teaspoons salt

Raspberry Filling

12 ounces fresh raspberries (about 3 cups) (see note)

¼ cup granulated sugar

1¼ teaspoons cornstarch

Sweet Glaze (page 214)

1. Scald milk in a medium saucepan over medium-low heat. (Milk will be scalded when foamy bubbles form around the edges of the pan and it almost starts to boil but doesn't.) Remove from heat and stir in butter and ¼ cup sugar until butter melts. Cool until lukewarm, about 10 minutes. Add instant yeast, stir to combine, then mix in egg.

2. In the bowl of a stand mixer fitted with the dough hook, add 2½ cups flour and salt and mix to combine. With mixer running on low, add liquid and mix until a soft dough forms. Knead until dough clears sides of the bowl, about 3 minutes, adding additional ½ cup flour a little at a time only if needed, until sticky but holding together.

3. Drizzle a little canola oil in a separate bowl and place the dough in it, turning it over to coat with oil. Cover the bowl with a clean towel and let rise until doubled, 1 to 2 hours.

Raspberry Sweet Rolls *(continued)*

Pro Tip: Always take multiple taste tests, especially when making food with fruit. You can't know if your food will taste good unless you sample it from start to finish. Freshly picked raspberries are much sweeter than store-bought berries, so take that into account when you add the sugar. Store-bought berries may need a little more sugar to get the sweet taste you're craving.

4. Just before rolling out dough, prepare raspberries by gently folding the berries, remaining ¼ cup sugar, and cornstarch together in a large bowl. Grease a 9x13-inch pan, line with parchment paper, and grease paper.

5. On a lightly floured surface, roll out dough to a 14x10-inch rectangle. Spread raspberry mixture all the way to the edges of the dough and, starting from the long side, roll up dough into a tight cylinder. Using unflavored dental floss, a serrated knife, or a bench scraper, slice into 1½-inch rolls.

6. Place cut rolls in prepared pan, cover with a clean towel, and let rise until doubled, about 1 hour. Do not over-rise.

7. Bake at 350 degrees F. 25 to 35 minutes, until golden and baked through.

8. Cool until warm, then spread generously with Sweet Glaze.

NOTE: You can use frozen raspberries in place of fresh as long as you make sure the raspberries were not frozen in syrup or juices. Do not defrost berries before tossing with sugar and cornstarch in step 4. Because frozen berries have more juice, you may need to increase cornstarch to 1¾ teaspoons.

NOTE: This dough can be prepared through step 3 and stored, covered, in the refrigerator up to 24 hours. Allow dough to come back to room temperature before rolling it out. Never prepare the raspberries ahead of time.

Sweet Glaze

Time: 10 min

¼ cup butter, softened

3½ cups powdered sugar

1 teaspoon vanilla

¼ teaspoon salt

¼ to ½ cup milk or evaporated milk

In a large bowl, beat the butter with an electric hand mixer on high speed until smooth. Add powdered sugar, vanilla, and salt and beat on low speed until combined. Add milk, a little at a time, until desired consistency is reached.

INDEX

INDEX